And So
I Wrote Again

Susan C. Ratliff

PublishAmerica
Baltimore

First printing

ISBN: 1-4137-8177-2
PUBLISHED BY PUBLISHAMERICA, LLLP
www.publishamerica.com
Baltimore

Printed in the United States of America

And So I Wrote Again
(24 December 2004)

I lost a friend one day
He decided his own fate
From life he ran away
And forever marked the date
Sadness overwhelmed me
I couldn't handle the pain
I thought I'd lose my sanity
I needed a way to stay sane
So I picked up my pen
And I poured out my heart
I put all my emotions on paper again
And from this pain I did part

This book is dedicated to the memory of my friend

Robert R. Reincke
19 September 1966–24 July 2004

To his mother and my best friend

Dianna Baker

And to my psychologist for the last ten years,
without whom I never would have made it this long in life

Dr. Rita Kenyon-Jump, Ph.D.

~

On 24 July, 2004, a close friend of mine chose his own fate and left a large hole in this world. The sadness he caused so many is more than even he could have imagined. As I looked at this hole he left in so many hearts, I decided to once again pick up my pen and write.

~

Just a Thought Away
(September 2004)

I know my death came as a painful shock to you,
The worst of my pain and fear you never knew.
The nights were so long, they seemed to never end,
The pain was so bad—I felt I could never mend.
The sun no longer brought me the kind of joy
That it once did when I was just a young boy.
I believed my life was such a horrid mess,
But I felt too guilty to ever confess.
I had reached the point of being so far in debt,
And it seemed I was always causing you to fret.
The anger raged within my body so bad
And my mind—so much turmoil it had.
The evils of alcohol had a grip on me that day,
And the anger took over me in such a way.
You believe that I died—gone forever from you,
But actually I was born, given life anew.
I'm in God's arms, living in his home,
I will never again feel the need to roam.
All my pain is gone—never to return again,
I have finally found a peace that will never end.
I am never hungry, I never need a drink,
I'm free of the alcohol—I've found the missing link.
Please don't cry for me, I've finished my earthly journey,
I'm home in Heaven now, you've no more need to worry.
The Lord says I've earned my Angel wings,
He gave me a halo and Angel Dust and things.
I'm with you always now—I know you can feel me,
And you'll find me all around if you only believe it to be.
I'll wash your tears away with the rain,
I'll kiss you gently with the breeze.
I'll paint your smile with the flowers
And show you a rainbow to ease your pain.
I'll shine the moon over you at night if you please,
And the sunrises and sunsets will always be ours.

I will be with you always—do not fear,
In the thunder, you will find, my laughter you can hear.
I'll always be just a thought away
Until we meet again in Heaven one day.

In memory of Robert Ray Reincke
19 September 1966–24 July 2004

~

Rob's mom, Dianna, is my best friend, and she is hurting so much from Rob's decision. I wrote the next poem for her.

~

Dear God
(18 October 2004)

I have a friend that's so special to me
And she's carrying so much pain that I can see.
She feels she has failed at the game of life,
Failed as a mother in her child's life.
She lost her son to you in such a tragic way,
Now she blames herself each and every day.
The question "What if…?" leaves so much unanswered
And the "If only…" never gives a positive word.
I'd like to take away all her pain if only I could
And make her feel happy again like she should.
Tell her that in this world she is not alone,
All she ever has to do is pick up the phone.
I think she knows I'll always be there when she calls
And I'll do anything I can to pick her up when she falls.
But the pain she feels I alone cannot mend,
Even though she is my dearest friend,
So I've come to you on bended knee
And asked you to please help me see.
How can I ease the pain that she feels in her heart
And keep it from tearing her completely apart.
Please let her know that I'm always by her side
And from me, her pain, she doesn't have to hide.
Give me what I need to show her the way
And get her through each sad and lonely day.
Please give me what I need to stand by my friend
And give her what she needs to one day mend.

~

I remember well the phone call from my best friend saying her only son and eldest child had died by his own hand. She was devastated, emotional and in shock. She called just before I went to work on that Saturday night—it was the first time I had ever heard her cry. I wrote the next poem just a few hours later.

~

Rob Reincke
(24 July 2004)

You gave no warning of what the day would hold.
You gave no warning of how you felt so alone and cold.
So many people would have been there for you,
You had friends that were tried and true.
You left such a hole in the world today,
It's not enough to just accept fate this way.
So much pain you carried around inside,
You must have felt there was no place to hide.
Your pain has been taken from you this way
But you've left your mother's heart aching today.
You will be forever missed, a large hole in life,
An aching pain that cuts like a knife.
Nothing and no one will ever plug the hole,
The tears will forever pour from my soul.

~

August and September were busy taking care of things Rob had left behind. By October, the real pain started to hit me. Just before Halloween I had a day when I really missed Rob a great deal, to the point of tears that I didn't want to show. I was in such a struggle with my mind, wanting to join him, wishing I could have gone with him. I wished I could have saved him and yet at the time of his death I had no idea that he was even depressed. He had been at my new house helping me with the phone lines just a few days before, and I recall thinking how happy he seemed to be. Now, different thoughts were very strong—I felt the butterflies in my stomach, the adrenaline rush through my body and a physical response so strong that I wanted to end things right at that moment. However, I knew that if I was to give way to my emotions I would cause his mom so much pain—I couldn't be that selfish.

I love watching the sun rise and set. I close my eyes and feel the warm rays on my face that brings a vision to my mind. My vision is that of a silhouetted person on the beach, facing the water with the sun on the horizon casting reds and oranges throughout the sky. The person is feeling suicidal, struggling between life and death. The light of day represents life, and the dark of night represents death. The individual on the beach has to decide for themselves if they are watching a sunrise or a sunset.

~

I Will Not Cry
(27 October 2004)

I will not cry—I will not cry
I will not cry—I will not cry
It's okay for you to say goodbye—
I will not cry
From now until the day I die
I will not cry
I may be a very lonely guy—
But I will not cry
I'm telling the truth,
I cannot lie—
I will not cry
No matter how dark the sky—
I will not cry
No matter how hard you try—
You will not make me cry.
I will not cry.
Hear me now one more time as I say—
I will not cry—I will not cry
I will not cry—I will not cry

Cold Winter's Day
(27 October 2004)

The days still come and the days still go
But without you near the time passes so slow
Especially each long and lonely night
When the darkness closes in so tight
And the silence leaves me so cold
With only memories of you to hold
You may have found a way to escape the pain
But you left me standing here in a cold, hard rain
Who will provide me with shelter now
I must go on but I don't know how
You couldn't face another minute of the day
And yet you expect *me* to live on this way
How can you ask me to do what you could not
What were *you* missing that you think *I've* got
I'm no stronger or better than you
I can't do anything *you* couldn't do
Now I must live with this painful emptiness
Every day losing a little more of my happiness
Every day aching a little more
Trapped behind such a heavy door
Because *you* chose to end your life this way
And leave me alone on this cold winter's day

~

For the most part I expressed my emotions and ask my whys within my poetry, trying to find answers to so many questions I had.

~

Hurting and Haunted
(27 October 2004)

Death is a place where I've not been.
I know one day I'll go but I don't know when.
I've known the desire to live, but it doesn't last,
It always seems to fade away from me too fast.
Peace is something that I've rarely known,
Most often I feel the emptiness of being alone.
I long for those days of peaceful dreams,
My soul is so painfully empty it seems.
My arms ache to hold you tight,
My eyes strain to bring you into sight.
My ears listen—awaiting your whisper so sweet,
My hands long to feel your heart's rhythmic beat.
(A beat that breaks through the stillness of the night)
And still, for any little hint of you I fight.
How could you leave me here this way?
Why did you leave me alone to face the day?
Why didn't you stay to help me through,
Or at least find a way to take me with you?
I hope you found the peace that you sought
The day you brought your life to a halt.
But my pain grew so much deeper that day
When I saw you in that coffin that way.
Yes, you may have found the peace you desperately wanted,
But you left me alone, cold, hurting and haunted.
How dare you go and leave me here,
In this dark world of fear!?

~

I saw my psychologist on Thursday, October 28, and I really wasn't doing well. I couldn't promise her that I would not follow through with my own suicide. I knew it was not the answer, but the feelings were strong at times, sometimes too strong—they frightened me. The only way I could stop myself was to sit down and not allow myself to get up because it would have been too risky, I didn't know what I would do.

Friday, October 29, was not one of my better days either. I had slid slowly down into a depression—I really didn't care if I died that day, it would have been okay with me. I wondered why I continued to go on.

Saturday, October 30, I think I had hit a record low. Knowing Rob had ended his life almost made it easier for me, because I knew whatever happened after death, at least Rob would be there.

~

Why?
(30 October 2004)

What happened to you that day?
Why did you have to leave us that way?
Why didn't you take the time to say goodbye?
Why didn't you leave us a note as to why?
Was your life really so horribly bad
That you felt death was the only option you had?
So many have taken this path before you,
So many are still getting ready to.
How I wish I could know what you found there,
At that moment of death were you aware?
How did you overcome the fear?
How did you find the strength to leave here?
I long so to go where you've gone
But how do I know if it's wrong?
Is there truly peace after you die?
Even if *you* choose when to say goodbye?
Can we really just quit that way
And never feel the pain of another day?
How I wish I knew what you know now,
If it would be a good thing for me to go,
Make that leap into another land
And once again take you by the hand.

The Secrets of My Soul
(30 October 2004)

I cannot show the secrets of my soul to you
These desires that are so old and yet so very new
The darkness of the night has overcome me
The warm light of hope has ceased to be
Should I live on or should I let myself die
There are so many questions that start with why
I can feel myself drowning in my sorrow
I've lost all hope of a better tomorrow
As I lie here in bed tired but still awake
Trying to get past my painful heartache
I'm surrounded by a deep sorrow that fills the room
It holds me in this sadness like a tomb
It feels like there is no way out
My future carries so much doubt
I long to enter into an eternal sleep
To pull the cord and take that long leap
To leave the pain of this world behind
And ease all the torment in my mind
To calm this storm forevermore
And enter into death's door

~

Wanting to die and actually taking your own life are two different things. I believe there are more passive people in this world wanting to be dead than we know. Normally we only hear about the more assertive people, that actually complete or attempt to take their own life.

~

With Rob Again
(30 October 2004)

Rob took the final step out of here
He made his decision and fought the fear
He made up his mind and chose to die
He never even took the time to say goodbye

If he can do it then why can't I
Can you tell me just exactly why
Deep into the darkness I want to go
Even though it's a world I don't know

If only I could ask him what he found
If only he could still come around
Is he truly happy in the place where he has gone
Or was the decision he made all wrong

Did he find the peace he was looking for
Or has he stepped into a hell forevermore
I too am ready to die but do I dare
Not really knowing exactly what's out there

I wish somebody would decide this for me
And take away each painful memory
Send me there to be with Rob again
Send me around that dark, fearful bend

~

By the early morning hours of Sunday October 31st I had reached the point of tears and it had happened at work. It was a very stressful night, and with the mood I had been in lately, I just reached the point that I couldn't hold back the tears anymore, I felt like I was going to crumble soon.

~

I Cry
(31 October 2004)

Once again I've begun to cry
It's uncontrolled and I don't know why
My eyes fill then begin to overflow
My heart aches, I feel so low
The pain in my chest is so real
I wish this hurt I didn't have to feel
Has the time come yet for *me* to die
I believe the time has come for me to try
I think of all the pills and they tempt me so
Into a permanent sleep is where I want to go
Never again to face this life
Never again to feel the knife
That cuts my heart out of my chest
Causing the pain, the tears and all the rest
I want to dry these tears forever now
I want to die—please show me how

Make the World Go Away
(01 November 2004)

Dry the tears in my eyes
Find me answers for all the whys
Ease the aching pain in my heart
Help all this sadness to depart
Stop the shaking in my hands
Take me away to better lands
Steady my knees when I walk
Steady my voice when I talk
Lift this weight from my back
Give me the peace that I lack
Make the world go away
I don't want to live another day

I Would
(01 November 2004)

My heart aches
The pain cuts like a knife
I don't think I have what it takes
To survive the turmoil in life

All the tears in my eyes
I can't stop them from flowing
Nobody hears my painful cries
I don't know where I'm going

My heart bleeds so
The blood is bright red
There's no place to go
No reason to get out of bed

The peace that I once had
Is gone now, forever lost
I feel so sad
It's such a high cost

If only I could die
Leave this world for good
If only I had the courage to try
Then leave this world I would

~

For those of us that struggle with depression, the cycle is all too well known, you're happy then sad then happy again.

~

The Cycle
(01 November 2004)

I struggle with a deep desire to die
I know it's just a mood that will pass on by
The aching pain in my chest will eventually ease
But not before it brings me to my knees
My broken heart will one day mend
But it will also be broken again
The flood of tears will someday dry
But I'll never know exactly why
The tears will flow again one day
And once again I'll lose my way
Again I'll fight the desire to die
And again it will pass me on by
The cycle will continue on through life
This pain will often return to cut like a knife
One day I may lose at this game
Decide I just can't go on the same
Decide it's time to go to sleep
To escape this sadness that runs so deep
When that day comes to be
I'll put an end to me
And I hope you'll understand
I felt I was sinking in the sand
I'd done everything that I could
And I'd said everything that I should
I saw no other way out that day
I felt it was the only way
So please don't cry for me
I'm at peace now, don't you see?

Sleep
(01 November 2004)

Sleep is such a wondrous thing
I'm peaceful when I'm sleeping
To sleep land I love to go
Life is so much easier there you know
I don't want to hear a thing
But I also don't want to dream
My dreams turn to nightmares too fast
And my peacefulness doesn't last
I wake up soaked in sweat
Once all my hidden demons I've met
Then I get cold, chilled to the bone
And find myself frightened to be alone
But in a sleep that's sound
Before the nightmares come around
When my heart barely has a beat
And there are no demons to defeat
When my lungs barely exchange air
And my mind hasn't a single care
In a place where they have said
You are as good as being dead
That's where I'd like to stay
And never have to face another day

~

Unfortunately, migraines are something I have had to deal with since July 1993. Anybody who has ever suffered from migraines will understand this poem.

~

Migraines
(02 November 2004)

My head hurts so
You can't begin to know
It usually starts late at night
And really messes up my sight
It's like a steel rod passing through my head
And it doesn't help to just go to bed
The pain grows and grows
The worse it gets the longer it goes
A break from the pain never comes to be
It just completely takes over me
Soon my eyes fill with tears
And I become overwhelmed with fears
My stomach begins to get upset
No relief can I ever get
My arms begin to ache so bad
Someone to hold me I'm wishing I had
The loneliness has once again begun
And there isn't anyplace I can run
This is the point when I want to die
When I'm begging for answers as to why
Why must I live with this intense pain
What could I possibly have to gain
At this point I just need it all to end
I need this horrible pain to mend
I'll do anything to make it go away
Even if it means I have to die today

~

I've spent enough time working in emergency medicine and nursing home care to have an opinion on death and dying. I have seen the process more times than I can recall, and each one is different.

~

Goodnight
(02 November 2004)

Your eyes slowly relax and close
As you let go of your cares and woes
Your heart beats slower and slower
Your head drops down lower
You exhale one last time releasing the air
You no longer have a reason to care
You fade into a sleep, peaceful as can be
You quietly slip away from me
You lived your life well
You've no more stories to tell
A deep sleep has overcome you
You've nothing left to do
Goodnight my dear friend
Goodnight until we meet again

Dying
(02 November 2004)

It's time for you to sleep
To sleep ever so deep
As you lie there the process begins
Death's dark angel just grins
Your eyes close one last time
As I think of all the memories that are mine
Your mouth slowly drops open
As you slip around life's bend
Your lungs stop—you breathe no more
Your heart stops—my tears begin to pour
Your blood no longer flows
Your body no longer grows
All your vital organs are shutting down
The world falls silent to you
The bright lights change their hue
You slip into a world of darkness forevermore
Death has come knocking at your door
Your skin turns blue and cold
As your hand I continue to hold
We say goodbye one last time
Losing you is such a crime
Goodbye for now has been said
And now you are dead

~

Wednesday, November 3, I learned about self-mutilation. I had done some cutting and didn't remember doing it or understand why I had done it, but on this day I thought I understood it better. My psychologist says that when the emotional pain becomes too overwhelming then a person inflicts physical pain on themselves. I didn't understand this at first, but after a lot of thought I realized that physical pain is something you can see, you can make it bleed—like purging the soul—you can make it stop bleeding. You can see it healing and feel better when it is better. None of this is possible with emotional pain.

I was out of energy. I had an appointment with my psychologist, and she could see that I was just totally exhausted. For the first time in seven years I went in the hospital and requested a one-on-one because I needed to feel safe. Four days later I went home, and the next day I went back to work, but the struggle wasn't over.

~

The Way to Win
(20 November 2004)

My aching heart is heavy today
My eyes are full of tears
My mind is empty in a way
My chest is full from the years
My friends are all within reach
And yet I feel so far from each one
I'm just a grain of sand on the beach
Burning up under the hot sun
The joy is all around me here
But the pain is all I feel
My heart bleeds with fear
My arms bleed, I won't let them heal
My eyes leak, the tears overflow
My lungs collapse, the air is gone
The anxiety begins to grow
I know that cutting is wrong
But with the razor in hand
I begin to cut the skin
Against the pain I make my stand
But I'm not so sure this is the way to win

~

November 11—Veterans Day—I just had to write something for all our veterans in this country.

~

War
(11 November 2004)

We remember those that went before us to fight
We mourn those that died in the dark of war's night
We treasure those that are there now afraid
We pray for those that are yet to go that they don't fade
We honor those of every generation present, future and past
We build memorials to the great that their names may last
We miss those that have not returned from far away
We search for those we cannot find yet to this day
We work to keep those from ever being those again
We work to make the world our friend

~

The death of a pet is always a very painful thing, it has a way of ripping our heart out and leaving an empty ache in its place.

~

My Four-Legged Love
(12 November 2004)

You came to me when you were just a baby
And jumped on my arm and kissed me like a lady
You knew right away I was the one for you
And I knew right off no other would ever do
We grew up side by side for many years
You were always around to dry my tears
We slept each night snuggled in our bed
You always stayed right there by my head
When I was sad you brought me cheer
And when I was scared you chased away the fear
Year after year passed by us two
And our love continued to grow like it was new
Now the years are bringing you down
Pretty soon you won't be around
You lie in my arms too weak to move
But you've nothing left to prove
My tears fall down on your face
As you come to the end of your life's race
Close your eyes now, we'll be okay
You sleep until we meet again one day.

Innocent Child
(13 November 2004)

What happened to the innocent child
The little one so very meek and mild
The child so many people once knew
Do you still carry that child within you
If you take the bricks from your wall
If you could climb back up from that painful fall
If you were able to reach beyond your fears
And break free from those bloody years
Would that child of innocence still be
Would that child still smile back at me
'Tis just a dream ~ this I know
Back in time we can never go
That innocent child is forever gone
Buried beneath all the painful wrong.

~

The day after Rob died, his mom was at my house all day. In the evening we stepped out on the deck and watched the moon. It was big and bright, and I said, "Just think of the moon as Rob's big flashlight shining down on us and he'll always be here." That story ended up sticking and was passed on. To this day I still think of Rob every time I see the moon.

~

Up on Top the Moon
(13 November 2004)

No! Stop! Look into my eyes
Can you see the deep darkness
Can you hear all the painful cries
Can you feel this horrible emptiness
Can't you see that I'm lost
I've no energy left to fight
I've paid too high a cost
I've been swallowed up by the night
I know my leaving will make you sad
But please understand that I must go
I don't want you to be mad
I still love you, don't you know
But for now I want to say goodbye
I'll see you again real soon
When your time comes to die
We'll meet up on top the moon

I've Decided
(13 November 2004)

My eyes are so empty and cold
I feel lost way down in my soul
My heart's beating faster all the time
The walls are too high for me to climb
Can you put some warmth in my eyes
Can you free me from all these ties
Can you find me and lift me from this hole
Can you help me to reach my goal
I no longer wish to live
I've nothing left to give
I want to get out of this rain
I think I may have gone insane
You can't keep me here, you know
Now that I've decided it's time to go
It doesn't matter how hard you try
I've decided it's time for me to die

~

One day Dianna told me that for the first week or more after Rob died she kept calling his answering machine just so she could hear his voice. Remembering the sound of someone's voice seems so important to our memory, it's like if we can't hear their voice anymore then we are even closer to forgetting them completely.

~

Your Voice
(13 November 2004)

Your voice has left me here alone
The silence of your voice is such an empty tone
I try to remember your beautiful sound
Now that your voice no longer comes around
Your voice was once locked in my mind
But more and more, no trace of it can I find
I call out and listen for your returning echo
But you won't answer, I already know
I call out to you to please speak to me
I just want to hear your sweet melody
But the pain and tears have already told me so
The reality of your silence is all I'll ever know

~

One thing that makes a grieving person really angry is when somebody else says something like, "Forget it and get on with your life." Obviously this person has never felt such grief.

~

Grief
(13 November 2004)

I cannot simply get over it
I cannot simply say it does not fit
It's not something I can merely go around
Or dig a deep tunnel underground
It is not something I can build a bridge over
Or wish it away with a four-leaf clover
It is not something I can avoid forever
It is not something I can forget, not ever
It brings about so much fear
It takes me so far away from here
It floods me with so many tears
It overcomes me in sorrow as it nears
I cannot just pass it by
It will never just simply die
It will be there forevermore
I've no chance but to pass through the door
There's only one thing for me to do
It is something I must walk through
I must cry the tears and feel the pain
I must scream and yell and go insane
It is grief and there is only one thing to do
I must jump in and pass through
When I reach the other side one day
My feet will hurt and my shoes will be worn away
And even though, at times, I may take a dive
I know this is something I will survive

~

I think as parents we tend to feel responsible for our children's actions regardless of how old they are. But the truth of the matter is that they are individuals with the power of a free will.

~

You Can Teach Your Children
(13 November 2004)

You can teach your children well while they grow
But you can't teach them everything they'll need to know
You can teach them the right way in life to go
But you don't know what demons wait in their shadow
You can bounce them up and down on your knee
And teach them what it takes to be truly happy
You can teach them what to do when they are mad
And how to live through times that are sad
You can give them your very best
And teach them how to handle stress
You can put love and kindness in their heart
And hope that it will never depart
Yes, you can teach your children well while they grow
But you can't teach them everything they'll need to know
You can't mend their heart when it is torn
You can't stop the evil once it's born
You can't make them save a single dime
Even if you did all the time
You can't always protect them in your hands
You can't keep them from traveling to foreign lands
You can't keep them from breaking your heart
You can't keep them from tearing your world apart
You can't make them live when they choose to die
You can't keep them from ever saying goodbye

Evil Deed
(13 November 2004)

I can't stand the pain anymore
So I turn and go through another door
This room is dark and strange to me
I'm shocked by all the things I see
All of a sudden I feel this need
I want to do this painful deed
I take the razor in my hand
And I venture out to a new land
Slowly I begin to cut my arm
Yes, I'm causing myself harm
I slice until it begins to bleed
I find myself enjoying this evil deed
I don't understand what I've found
But I like it when the urge comes around
Now, the marks are something I must hide
Or people will know that next is suicide

~

On November 14 I was at work and found it very difficult to stay there. Usually work is a good place for me when I'm feeling down, it's like a mental escape to get wrapped up in work, but not this night. My emotions were building up inside me, I could feel the pressure in my chest, it was like a dull ache. I could feel the flood of tears behind my eyes wanting to come out, but they were unable to. My arms ached in an empty kind of way, wanting, needing to be held. I had a desire to bleed as though a physical release could also work as an emotional release. I felt the deep desire to curl up in the dark, pull the covers over my head, hibernate in the dark warmth created there and cry until there wasn't a single tear left in my body. My emotions were like a flood building at the gate, screaming to get out, screaming for somebody to open the gate, to release these emotions before I went insane. The lack of feeling loved or needed clashing against the strong sadness, the lonely, empty pain. I wondered how I would get through, how I would survive.

~

Overwhelming Emotions
(14 November 2004)

I feel all the tears building up inside
All the bad emotions that I try to hide
The pressure in my chest builds more and more
I don't know what it's all in there for
The tremors in my body flow up and down
There doesn't seem to be any way around
All these emotions that are so strong
I know this has to be completely wrong
I need a way to ease the pain
I'm starting to feel a little insane
My eyes fill with overwhelming tears
My body fills with overwhelming fears
My mind fills with overwhelming doubt
My emotions scream, looking for a way out
The tears finally begin to flow
I don't want anybody to know
There has to be someplace I can hide
Until I get out all this stuff inside
Would you please pull me under your wing
Would you please protect me from everything
Would you please dry my tears
And find a way to ease my fears
I need someone now more than ever
I need someone to protect me forever

Let Me
(14 November 2004)

I'm screaming inside
So many tears I hide
My heart aches so bad
I've lost all the love I had
The blood pours from my soul
I'll never again be whole
Can't anybody see
How can it be
I just don't know why
I just want to die
I can't stop this pain
I can't get out of this rain
Stop my lungs and still my heart
Stop this pain from ripping me apart
Let me go to sleep forevermore
Let me pass through death's door

A Reason Why
(14 November 2004)

Does there always have to be a reason why
Does it always have to be something we can justify
Does there always have to be a reason to say goodbye
Is there always a reason why you should die
Does there always have to be a reason to cry
Does there always have to be a low after the high
Is there ever a good reason for the tear in your eye
Does it always have to be so wrong to lie
Do we always have to fail when we try
Is it always wrong to be so terribly shy
Does the desert always have to be so hot and dry
Does it always have to be impossible for people to fly
Is there always something a poem must signify
Does there always have to be a reason why

~

Scars are something we all have, and the older we get, the more we have. Most people can look at their scars and tell a story for each one. Each is like a chapter in their own book of life.

~

Scar Tissue Tattoos
(14 November 2004)

I have these scars on my being
Some that people aren't seeing
That tell a story of time
It's a story of mine
Some I remember how I got
Some I simply do not
Some are funny to recall
Some I wish I didn't remember at all
There's the one on my knee
From when I fell out of the tree
And the one on my arm
That didn't really do much harm
The one from the dog bite
The one from that dark night
The one from my stubbed toe
And this one—I don't know
There's one from the fishing pail
And the one from that rusty nail
There's the one from the toboggan trip
And this one here on my hip
The one next to my eye
And the one that made me cry
These are my tattoos, you see
Of my life's legacy
Memories etched in my skin
Memories of a long-lost friend
Memories of my childhood
And memories I've never understood
But these scar tissue tattoos of mine
Tell the story of my lifetime.

Darkest of All Nights
(15 November 2004)

I step out into the darkness
And the cold night's stillness
It's one of the darkest nights
With the ever so distant city lights
I breathe in the crisp cool air
As I notice there's not a cloud anywhere
I'm awed by the starlit sky
The stars are so far away and high
The moon is full and round
And there isn't the slightest sound
The trees are covered with frost
And most of their leaves have been lost
I stand here alone in the night
With the loneliness I must fight
And as I let out a deep sigh
I wonder once again why
Why am I here without you
And I wipe away a tear or two.

This Is Where I Come
(15 November 2004)

I drive out to the cemetery to see you
Walking through the grass and morning dew
The sun is just appearing in the morning sky
Chasing the night away as it rises high
I approach the spot where your body lies
The place where we all said our goodbyes
The stone on this spot has your name and dates
And an empty flower vase sits and waits
To hold today's fresh-cut flowers for you
This is where I come to honor you
To remember you, miss you and cry too
Your body is here beneath this ground
Where I stand and wander around
But your spirit and soul are in another place
This is only the end for the human race
You are an angel now with golden wings
You've gone beyond the world of material things
I can feel you with me everywhere I go
Your gentle presence I continue to know
Even though we are worlds apart
I will always feel you in my heart
I turn now from this place and walk away
But I know I'm not leaving you behind
You're still with me this and every day
You're still with me in my heart and mind

~

With our country currently at war in Iraq, our young Americans are living and dying in a horrible place. While many people don't support the war, I would hope they could at least find it in themselves to support the human beings our country has sent over there.

~

Our Freedom Holders
(16 November 2004)

They stand united as one
Side by side beneath the hot sun
They are the American soldiers
They are our freedom holders
They carry something special within
They will carry it to the end
Strangers from across the States
Now responsible for each other's fates
They stand their ground as a mighty force
Filled with honor from an undying source
They are made up of heroes of every kind
More courage you'll never find
They live and die side by side
By an honor code they do abide
They will never leave a man behind
They live by the oath that they signed
They are our guardian angels, you see
They know that freedom isn't free
Awake, on duty, while we safely sleep
Silently, unnoticed, our safety they keep
You may not like the battles and wars
But don't betray the ones that even our scores
They risk their life for us every day
And they deserve our respect in every way

Soldiers
(16 November 2004)

They are tired and sweating, moving fast as they can
They were dodging enemy fire while they ran
Trained young American fighting men
Together in a small detail of ten
Grenades blowing and bullets flying by
Men on a mission, praying they don't die
One soldier is hit and falls to the ground
Other brave men quickly gather round
Getting everyone out safe is on their mind
They know they can't leave a single one behind
The blood pours from him fresh and red
An arm just hanging by a vessel like a thread
His comrades pick him up still on the run
Moving in an even rhythm like they were all one
The wounded soldier looks through his tears
At his rescue team calming all his fears
He smiles and says, "I knew you'd come for me."
Then closes his eyes and faces his destiny
Soldiers return from war every day
Looking at life in a different way
Seeing friends die brings mental torment
These aren't the young boys that we sent
They've fought the war and seen the ruin
Their courage and dedication has been proven

~

What do we do for the people in this world that are emotionally lost? How many of us even know how to spot somebody that is lost in their own world of torment?

~

Anybody
(16 November 2004)

Can anybody see
That this is me
Does anybody know
Where I should go
Will anybody take a walk
And listen to me talk
Will anybody stand
And hold my hand
Will anybody wipe my tears
And calm all my fears
Can anybody tell me why
I often sit and cry
Can anybody ease my pain
And keep me from going insane
Does anybody know my name
And from where I came
Can anybody tell me the cost
Of my being so lost
Can anybody help me today
And show me the way
Are there any angels up above
That can show me some love
Is there anybody out there tonight
That can hold me tight
I feel so cold and alone
My heart is a melting stone

~

Have you ever gone and pulled out the old photos when you were lonely? They bring back memories that make you smile, laugh and even cry. Unfortunately they also tend to make you a little more lonely than you already were.

~

Pictures
(16 November 2004)

Pictures in my house hanging on the wall
All the different memories that I recall
From the little babies that I know
To the ones I love that are so very old
Birthdays, holidays and everything in between
All the lovely things that I've seen
All the happy times, the trips and the joys
Everything pictured there since I was a boy
Some are people I've not spoken to in a year
Some are people I'll always be near
Some are people who have moved far away
Some are people I just saw the other day
Some of them have shared my tears
Some of them have banished my fears
And some of them have passed away
While others still live on to this day
All of these pictures ~ memories of mine
Are what's carried me through time

A Solitary Stone
(16 November 2004)

He was the best friend I ever had
The day he died was so very sad
If only dying had not been his choice
I've often wished I could hear his voice
For years and years we've lived as one
Daring to do anything the other had done
He was like a brother, he was my true friend
I don't know why his life had to come to an end
I thought I knew him, knew him well
I thought I'd be able to catch him when he fell
But there was no warning that he gave
No chance for him to be saved
One day the pain became far too great
And he decided to choose his own fate
So now I'm left here all alone
Kicking around a solitary stone

~

Holidays can be one of the most difficult times after you have lost somebody you love. Traditions are broken, and every time you open your eyes you see something else that brings back another sharp reminder of your painful loss.

~

Holiday Memories
(17 November 2004)

Once again the holidays are here
But they are so terribly different this year
All the memories of holidays past
Fly through my mind so incredibly fast
There are so many happy memories of those years long ago
But the holidays will never be like that again, I know
I wrap myself in smiles and holiday cheer
I do my best not to let them see my fear
I stack the gifts and tie the bows
I hang the lights so the tree glows
But there aren't as many gifts as there used to be
Because there's somebody special missing for me
I can't just put their memory out of my mind
Every time I turn around there's something I find
That makes me wish my somebody was here
And I have to wipe away a tear
Somehow I have to get through these days
I just wish there were other ways

The Sound of Silence
(19 November 2004)

I'm feeling so happy and free of doubt
I just want to scream and shout
There is so much noise in this place
It fills every crevice of this space
It is full of happy and joyful cheer
The sound of silence is never heard here
You are here with me holding my hand
And we are having all the fun that we can
But then...
I'm feeling so lonely and full of doubt
I haven't the energy to scream and shout
The silence echoes so bad in this place
As I stand here in this dark empty space
It is full of my sweet memories of you
Your being gone has left me feeling so blue
I've never felt so terribly alone before
My heart just aches for you more and more
The sound of silence has me trapped in a tomb
The sound of silence will be my doom

Day Is Done
(19 November 2004)

See the bright red glow of the sky
Colors emitted from the day's sun
This day has now begun to die
This day can't ever be another one
The land has fallen into a dark shadow
The night has nearly overcome everything
Our day's memories begin to softly echo
I begin to feel the cold of the night that's near
Somehow I have to make it through this alone now
The night's darkness closing in on me, bringing fear
I let you slip away from me somehow
I don't want to be without you here
I don't want to stand alone looking up to the moon
Knowing that you are gone forevermore
I want to leave this world real soon
And be with you again on the other side of life's door

Do We Dare
(20 November 2004)

I can see you're hurting so terribly bad
I wish the right words for you I had
Can you see I'm hurting and crying too
Do you know there are at least us two
I know there are more like us around
If you listen you can hear their crying sound
I wish I could find you some happiness here
I know you'd do anything to give me cheer
So what do you think we should do
I'm sorry that I don't know for you
Just because we are not the only ones
Doesn't ease the weight—it's like ten tons
Would you come and hold me tight
If I agree to hold you through the night
Would you say that you love me too
If I say how much I love you
Would you agree to end our pain
And keep us both from going insane
I have a gun here in my hand
That will take us to a new land
A land where we are at peace in our heart
A land where all this sadness will forever part
A land where we can be together forever
And we won't cry again, no, never
Can you do this for me, take me there,
And I'll do this for you, do we dare

I'm Sorry
(21 November 2004)

I'm sorry you have so much pain
I guess I didn't know
How much you'd go insane
By my letting go
I never wanted to hurt you
I wish I could give you a hug somehow
And tell you it's okay to be blue
But I'm so much happier now
I have a peace within my soul
It's something that will always be
I no longer feel like I'm in a dark hole
I have finally been set free
Maybe I should have left a note some way
But I probably wouldn't have been nice to you
I was in such a horrible fit of rage that day
That I took my life away from you
Know that I had an angel with me
He was right there when I died
And know that I'm the angel you can't see
I'm always right here by your side
You have to hang on down there now
Even though you feel you're doing it alone
You have to finish what I didn't somehow
It's not time yet for you to come home
I'm sorry you hurt so bad
I'm sorry you cry for me
I'm sorry you lost what you had
But I was feeling so empty
I don't want you to continue in pain
I don't want you to cry anymore
I need you to find shelter from the rain
And let your spirit soar
I'll be right here waiting for you
When you can't take it anymore
And I'll be there to meet you
When you pass through death's door

One Minute More
(22 November 2004)

The sky is a little darker to me tonight
And the lights are a little dimmer without you
The moon is a little smaller at that height
My walk a little longer and harder to do
My home is a little farther away
The tunnels are a little deeper
And the mountains are a little higher today
The waves are getting a little steeper
Each tree seems a little taller than the last
And my path seems a little bit tougher
My eyes a little more teary than the past
My chest is a little tighter as I suffer
My heart is a little heavier without you
And my pain a little sharper than before
I wish I knew what I could do
To see you one minute more

~

I met somebody on the Internet who said her husband would soon be deploying to Iraq, I wrote this poem for them.

~

Bring Him Home Safe
(22 November 2004)

There is this handsome man,
I love him more than myself, you know
But it's his time to take a stand
They have called him up to go

He took an oath before God and country
That he would protect our freedom for free
That he would be there when called to be
Even if it means being far away from me

Our country is in a horrible war
Off in another country, in another land
Our freedom is worth fighting for
Off in that world surrounded in sand

He is a strong honorable man
And although he must leave me behind
My memories will go with him to that land
And every night in his dreams he'll find

I'll be there with folded hands
Praying to God to bring him home again
And protect him when he makes his stand
Asking God, "My love to him please send"

In the meantime time I'll be here
Keeping this world going well
Trying to contain all my fear
That he might be the one who fell

Dear God, bring him home safe to me
With his love and softness still
Put a Guardian Angel there he can see
And give him a strong will

77

~

I've heard all things happen for a reason. Based on that I find myself searching for the reason Rob reached a point in life where he felt so hopeless that he chose to end his life at such an age. The only thing I can come up with is this—Rob died leaving a hole in my heart. I became so sad that I felt the need to write—you are now reading what I've written, and perhaps that will save a life. What other reason could there be for God to call this Angel home?

~

Why You Had to Die
(23 November 2004)

As I lie here listening to the night
The cars outside my window quickly passing by
I watch the walls reflecting each passing headlight
And I'm wondering why it was you that had to die
Why did you leave me here all alone
And then my pillow catches another falling tear
As I lie here waiting for a call on the phone
My body is overcome with sadness and fear
I know you're the Angel here with me
Watching over me as best you can
I just wish you were something I could see
Something I could feel with my hand
But I know your touch so well
My heart slows and calmness comes over me
I know you're right here—I can tell
Please stay—don't leave me cold and lonely
When I wake in the morning you'll be gone
But with the thought of you I'll smile and sigh
I'll know that what I felt couldn't be wrong
And again, I'll wonder why you had to die

I Was Holding You
(23 November 2004)

I close my eyes and I think of you
I pull an image of you into my mind
I can see your beautiful eyes of blue
Your features are all uniquely one of a kind
Your dimples stand out so well
When you smile that way that you do
I almost forget that it was you who fell
And that I'm desperately missing you
I watch the sun reflect off your golden hair
And I notice that against the bright sky you glow
I can tell you no longer have a care
You're happy and peaceful now, I know
Your image is so real to me
And I reach out to touch and hold you
But I'm snapped back into reality
And I realize I'm still here without you
Oh, I dreamed such a sweet dream
I touched you and kissed you so true
We were together again it did seem
Yes—I was holding you

A Dream
(23 November 2004)

I opened my eyes and saw the gate
I was standing in the clouds up above
I knew this must be Heaven and my fate
I wanted to see the one who stole my love

There was a movement—a shadow of some kind
I thought of all those I had loved before
The ones that had gone and left me behind
I wondered if I too had passed through death's door

Toward the gate and the shadow I ran
I was hoping and wishing it was you
My heart raced and the tears began
It was almost like I knew

Yes, you were there waiting for me
With your halo and robe of white
You were so lovely to see
I wanted to hold you so tight

But just as I reached out to touch you
I was blinded by the brightest light
Once again I opened my eyes to see you
But you were gone, gone with the night

~

Wouldn't it be a wonderful thing if every time somebody we loved left this world somebody else we would love came into our lives, and that we would see the connection instantly? Wouldn't it be a wonderful thing if all our sorrow was evenly balanced with all of our joy?

~

The Life Cycle
(23 November 2004)

A man lies in his bed—frail, crippled and old
A woman lies in her bed—young, vibrant and bold
As the pain comes from inside the man he moans
As the sharp pain stabs the woman, she groans
The man slowly inhales the air
Working hard to fill his chest
The woman pants heavily, very much aware
The pain won't give her a rest
Then an infant wails, proclaiming life
The man's heart slows as he looks at his wife
Ten little fingers and toes wiggle about
As you hear the joyous people shout
An Angel of Death takes the man's hand
And an Angel of Life lets go again
The man slowly slips away and is gone from here
The infant slowly slips in and appears without fear
Two souls passing in time quietly
Life and Death both whisper softly
So the cycle of life begins
And the cycle ends

True Love
(24 November 2004)

To be touched in such a way
The soft, tender touch of a man
His soft kiss at the start and end of each day
Just knowing that he is my greatest fan
To be loved from another's heart so true
To be held in a way that calms my fears
To live in a world where our love always grew
To feel his gentle hand brush away my tears
To lay my weary head on his chest
And be held in his arms so strong
To be able to be completely at rest
To know these feelings are not wrong
To trust a man with all my heart
To know he would die to protect me
To love a man who is dedicated from the start
To know a man that would never hurt me—
That would be to know true love
And oh—how I would like to know true love

~

I wrote this next poem based on the number of people lost to suicide and the number of people that survive suicide attempts, even when the situation and method seem to be identical.

~

Two People
(24 November 2004)

Give me an acceptable answer if you dare
Tell me why and make me aware
Two people in the same situation
Two people with the same information
In the end only one has to die
Can anybody explain to me why
Why does one die and one live
Did one have more than the other to give
Did one have a stronger will to survive
Is that why only one is left alive
Was fate in charge of them that day
Is that why it happened just that way
Only one lives, only one dies
And they both leave us with so many whys
Questions where answers can't be found
Questions where the whys just compound
Two lives traveling the same road
Two people carrying the same load
But one ends up at death's door
And the other lives on forevermore

Some Days
(24 November 2004)

The sun comes up and the sun goes down
The world turns round and round
People come into this world on good days
And people leave this world in bad ways
Some people just love to talk
And some people just love to walk
The trees grow taller and taller
While the lakes get smaller and smaller
Some animals and insects know how to fly
And some have to use their legs to get by
Every day it seems that somebody dies
And every night it seems that somebody cries
Sometimes the clouds are thick and gray
And sometimes the sky is clear all day
Some people fall in and out of love so fast
And for some, their first love is their last
Some days this world is very sad
And some days this world is very mad
Some people believe in forever
And some people don't believe, ever
All the ups and downs, ins and outs, and whys
And in the end it's nothing but good-byes

~

I wrote the next poem as a symbol of true friendship right to the end. A lifelong friendship is such a wonderful thing and yet so rare.

~

Let's Make a Pact
(24 November 2004)

Let's make a pact, you and me
We can do it together—you'll see
You help me and I'll help you
We can do anything, us two
I'll watch your back and you watch mine
Everything will be just fine

It wasn't long until the word was sent
And off to war the two men went
We have to keep our heads down
Stay real close to the ground
The bullets are coming close by
But I promise you we won't die
You help me and I'll help you
We can survive anything, us two

It wasn't long until the battle was won
And everybody went home—they were done
The days came and the days went
They lived in a house and they lived in a tent
One day they were rich, the next they were poor
And then they both came to death's door

Let's make a pact, you and me
We can do it together, you'll see
You help me and I'll help you
We can do anything, us two

Sundown
(25 November 2004)

The sun is nearly down
The day is nearly done
The sky has no sound
Another battle has been won

Three shadows walking side by side
Holding each other up as they walk
Remembering all those who died
Mostly silent, very little talk

Loaded guns in their hand
Eyes still full of fear
Wounded bodies cover the land
Soldiers slowly dying here

Blood has been spilled today
Even though they fought their best
Many died along the way
Many still can't seem to rest

A time when wining is still sad
A time when dying is never good
A time when everything is bad
A time when things are not understood

We won the battle this time
But it's a battle we shouldn't have fought
And there is no purpose to this rhyme
Even though one is often sought

~

With the holidays fast approaching people seemed to grow more and more depressed. The next year would be full of firsts—his first birthday he didn't live to see, the first Halloween he didn't dress up for, the first Thanksgiving with a hole in the family, and worst of all, the first Christmas without Rob here.

~

Another Holiday
(25 November 2004)

Another holiday has come to me
Another holiday without you
I wish it were just another day
But I still wouldn't know what to do

I wondered for weeks how I'd get through
Flooded with memories of when you were here
Of when you sat around the house too—
It's so much harder this year
I don't ever want to forget anything
Any memories of your life

I want to always remember everything
Even when it cuts me like a knife
Didn't you know that I loved you so
You are such a part of me
Why did you choose to go
Why did this have to be

Another holiday is gone
I made it through the day
But without you it just felt so wrong
I wish there could have been another way
All day you were on my mind
Once I even started to cry

Everybody tried to be so kind
But nobody could answer why
Why did you leave us here
Why did you leave me alone
I can't find any holiday cheer
Because I know you'll never come home

Another holiday will come and go
And I'll still hurt from missing you
There will always be a memory I know
Something you used to say or do
Something I just can't get past
Something that will make me cry

The pain of your loss will always last
And I'll always hurt until the day I die
Only then will I stop missing you
Only then will I be whole again, like new
Only then will I know what to do
Because only then will I once again find you

~

The second bird I ever took in was a four-month-old Green Quaker. I chose to name her Pickles because she seemed to get herself into a pickle often as well as her being green. I also needed a universal name, because at the time I didn't know if she was a he or she. Pickles would prove to be one of my greatest friends. She spent most of her time preening me, nestled in my hair, or sleeping with her body snug against my face. Pickles stands guard when I am afraid, entertains me with her silliness when I'm sad, chases me out of bed when I'm depressed and loves me when I am lonely. We have been together nearly nine years.

~

Pickles (The Bird)
(27 November 2004)

I remember the first time I saw you, it was over eight years ago
I wasn't real sure just what to do, there was so much I didn't know
But it didn't take long for me to fall in love with you
Right off I could see, it didn't matter what I knew
You would teach me just what to do

On my shoulder you always sat and loved me all day and night
It didn't take long for you to get fat, eating everything in sight
You loved to drink my Mountain Dew and eat everything that I ate
Even though it wasn't good for you,
You'd always perch on my plate

In the car you would ride on the swing I hung for you
On the rearview mirror with pride,
Watching everybody watching you
At night when I would watch TV,
You would sleep on the back of my chair
Keeping watch over me, letting me know you cared
And when it was time for bed, you were always right there
Listening to whatever I said, snuggled down in my hair

And when the really bad times I had,
You would wipe away each tear
You knew when I was sad and you tried to give me cheer

When I wanted to stay in the bed all day and not face anyone
You would run across me like I was dead,
Screaming at me until you won
And I would have to get up, but with you protecting me
I had no reason to hide, not with you at my side.

95

~

Have you ever noticed the best place to hide your worst emotions is in the dark? Nobody can see your red, swollen eyes, the tears that stain your face or the extreme sadness your expression shows.

~

Sadness Inside of Me
(29 November 2004)

It's 3 a.m. and I sit here all alone
In a chair in the midst of my own home
It's dark—every light is turned out
So much turmoil inside makes me want to shout
My thoughts echo in the silence of the night
I know there's so much that isn't right
I can't control all the painful tears
A reflection of my life's many years
The house is quiet—nobody else is awake
No one knows that my daily smile is a fake

I know that before the rising of the sun
I must dry my tears, calm my fears and be done
This painful pressure in my chest must fade away
Before the start of a brand-new day
I can't let anybody see
All the sadness inside of me

The Rain
(29 November 2004)

How I wish the rain
Could wash away my tears
Ease all of my pain
And calm all of my fears
I wish it could penetrate my chest
And wash out my heart
Let me take a long rest
And stop what's tearing me apart

How I wish the rain
Could wash all the blood away
Keep me from going insane
And give me a better day
Wash the sadness out of my eyes
And wipe away my past
Take back all the lies
And make the happiness last

~

This year we had our first big snow on Thanksgiving Day.

~

The First Snow
(29 November 2004)

The air has turned cold
Everything is frozen now
The trees are bare and old
Only a few things survive somehow
The clouds are thick and gray
The rain turns to snow
It's nearing the end of the day
This is the first snow, don't you know
The snow comes down, covering the ground
Getting deeper with each flake that falls
The frozen night has no sound
There's no children throwing snowballs
No sleds flying down the hill
There's no funny-looking snowmen
But there is ice gathering on the window sill
There's no more flowers to tend
But it's time to get the shovels out
And clear off the driveway
The children begin to shout
With the breaking of a new day
And everybody is happy
With the first snow they see

A Life Erased
(29 November 2004)

Shots ring out
Bullets fly true
People shout
Death is due
Falling to the ground
Blood spurting red
The heart has no sound
The boy is dead
The silence of night
Tears begin to fall
Fear in sight
Mourners call
Empty ground
Casket full
Flowers abound
Emotions dull
Dirt thrown in
Headstone placed
Lost in sin
A life erased

The Night
(29 November 2004)

The night is too long
It never seems to end
My feelings are all wrong
I know I'll never mend
It's a cold, cold night
And I am here all alone
There's no relief in sight
Nobody to hear me moan
No mending my broken heart
And no drying my tears
There's nobody who sees
That I'm falling apart
And nobody to calm my fears
Why won't the darkness fade away
And let the sun shine through
I need to see the light of day
And feel the warmth of it too
Save me from this dark hole
Won't you please reach down for me
Save my poor aching soul
And teach me to be free

~

Cam was my high school sweetheart. We had an on-again-off-again relationship for the last 22 years—perhaps some day we will get it right.

~

Cam
(02 December 2004)

We met so young and so long ago
Back then so little did we know
We had no idea what await
How our love would be played by fate
We have been together and apart
So many times we've had a broken heart
I know we were meant to be
I know you really love me
You know I really love you
But something always separates us two
You have a daughter and a son
But children—I have none
You were married one time before
But I've never loved anyone else more
Than I've loved you since the day
That you crossed my pathway
Someday we will be
I'm sure of you and me
Someday you'll knock on my door
And say that you'll love me forevermore

~

I have four nephews, with the oldest, Jon, 18 years old, belonging to my brother and his wife. The youngest are currently 7, one is my sister's son, the other my brother's son, and in the middle is Mark, 15 years old currently. I wrote a poem for each of them after Jon told me he wanted to join the Army.

~

To My Nephew Jon
(02 December 2004)

My little boy I love is all grown
And beginning to reap what he has sown
You've stepped through that door
And become an adult forevermore
Your just as sweet and kind
As any man I could ever find
Now you're ready to take the next leap
And it's one that will be very steep
You say you want to be a soldier
You want the army to be your molder
I am so very proud of you
I know you'll be great at what you do
In your uniform you'll stand so tall
I just pray to the Lord you never fall
The life of a soldier is a dangerous one
After boot camp and your training is done
They may send you far away overseas
To a place with only sand—no trees
Our country is in the midst of a war
And a debate of what we are fighting for
Young soldiers are dying every day
Dying in every kind of way
I pray that you don't have to go
That death is something you won't know
But if you do find yourself there
Keep your eyes and ears open everywhere
Try not to be afraid every single day
Try to have some fun in some way
And if a fellow soldier falls from your side
Stop and help him, his fears to hide
Never leave a man behind
Never erase them from your mind
And if the time comes for you to die
Remember that it is okay for a man to cry

To My Nephew Mark
(02 December 2004)

You are growing, soon a man to be
Somebody special for all the world to see
You have so much potential in you
I know you'll be good at whatever you do
Life has so much in store
There'll always be another door
Something more to be done
Something where you're the only one
You'll have kids of your own one day
And you'll have to guide them along the way
I know you'll have a wife that will care
Because you have so much love to share
There'll be days that are hard to get through
And days where you will always find something new
You are going to be a wonderful man
And I will always be your number one fan
Cling to your family and friends forevermore
They'll put the wind under your wings so you can soar
The lessons in life are never easy or free
But don't be afraid to be on bended knee
Ask for guidance in all that you do
And you'll be an excellent you
Never be afraid to let yourself cry
And never be afraid to ask why
A man who shows emotion is hard to find
But you're man enough to be just that kind

I Have Seen
(03 December 2004)

I have seen the soldier wounded and dead
I have seen the blood flowing fresh and red
I have seen the bullets close as they fly
Hitting and missing as they go by
I have seen the joy and the sadness
I have seen the dark eyes of loneliness
I have seen the soldiers' fearful eyes
I have seen the wounded as he cries
I have seen the enemy close at hand
I have seen the ruin throughout the land
Yes, I have been to the land of war
I have stood with a pal at death's door
I have held and fired a gun
I have taken the life of someone
I have walked through the lands so muddy
I have done it alone and with a buddy
I have felt the sun boiling hot
And I have smelled the stench of the rot
I have died inside again and again
I have been where many have not been
I have seen what others have not
I have memories I wish I'd forgot
I've lived on into the by and by
It was not my time yet to die
But while my body continues to fight
My mind escapes forever into the night

~

After Rob died his mom really went through all the emotions over and over. Sometimes our friendship would feel the strain, but we always managed to get through somehow.

~

I've Upset You
(03 December 2004)

Once again I've upset you and I don't know why
It just seems like no matter how hard I try
I'm always doing something that's not quite right
It seems I constantly struggle and fight
Trying to be there by your side
And my own emotions I try to hide
I'm doing my best to support you
In everything that you do
But once again I've done something wrong
Will we ever again sing that song
Back when times were happy and life was good
Back when you were a little more easily understood
Back before you started always asking why
Back before Rob made the choice to die
I know for a long time yet you'll be sad
Because you no longer have what you once had
But all I've ever wanted was to help—you know
It's you that I always try to console
Won't you please help me along the way
While I try to support you from day to day
Together, the two of us, we can do this, you know
It's just not an easy way to go
But it can be done
You won't always have to run

My Daddy
(04 December 2004)

My daddy wears clothes like other people do
His friends and him all dress the same
He says it's because of his work—they all have to
Up on their chest they have their name
Momma says that Daddy has to go far away
And that he is not the only one
That tomorrow is going to be the day
And that they will all have to take a gun
He's going to play a game they call war
Far, far away from here, past the sea
And that he won't be coming through the door
Every night just to see her and me
They won't say it, but I know it's true
Somebody always dies when he takes his gun
They think I'm too young to have a clue
I just pray that my daddy's not the one

The Sacrifice Made
(04 December 2004)

Explosions all around, everywhere
Bullets flying past my head
I cannot run—I don't dare
Men screaming over the bloodshed
I touch my face with my hand
And then look to see my hand's blood red
There's fresh blood all over the land
Nothing around me but fire and smoke
Screaming men, flying bullets—death is near
I open my eyes to this view and choke
Down each side of my face runs a tear
Men dropping beside me left and right
All dead—never another breath to take
They all came here to be part of the fight
Their best effort they did make
But now they'll go home in a body bag
They'll see no special welcome parade
They'll each have their own toe tag
Few will truly know the sacrifice made
Few will realize those left behind
Left to live on all alone
Those who will never again find
That joy and peace again in their home

112

Died a Hero
(04 December 2004)

I'm sorry to tell you that he died
That he wasn't able to win his fight
But I must tell you what he said
Just before he died late that night
His friend was down and hurt real bad
Nobody could get help into him there
This made your son really very mad
And suddenly, very much aware,
He grabbed his gun and began to run
Straight through enemy fire he did go
Undaunted and brave, he was the only one
He wanted his friend to always know
He would never leave him behind
He picked him up and carried him through
But just before they were safe behind the line
A bullet broke and in his heart rang true
Your son died a hero, yes he did
That truth can't be changed or hid

~

Have you ever had the desire to escape your world? Even for just a little while, thought that it would be nice to be invisible?

~

I Want To...
(05 December 2004)

I want to get drunk, I want to get high,
I want to be numb, I want to fly.
I want to soar above the pain,
I want to slip under the insane.
I want to disappear—run away—
Leave everything behind for another day.
Invisible is what I want to be,
So nobody can see me.
Lift the pain from my heart,
It's tearing it all apart.
Leave me in total peace,
Make this world cease.
Bring comfort to my aching soul,
Put my useless body in a hole.
When I die do not cry for me
I'm at peace, be happy.

I'll Support You
(06 December 2004)

How do I convince you that my love is true
That I'll always stand by your side in whatever you do
How is it that I can be sure you know
That I'll always go wherever you go
I'll help you up when you fall down
I'll give you a smile in place of your frown
I'll dry your tears when you cry
I'll be there to encourage you when you try
I'll catch you when you stumble and fall
I'll come running any time you call
How do I make you truly believe me
Believe that I will always help you see
Which is the best way for you
And that I'll support everything you do

~

"Frozen Bird" is a tale about a person happy and free that suddenly falls into the hole of depression and eventually ends his life.

~

Frozen Bird
(06 December 2004)

Just a little bird down in the snow
Frozen and wounded—fallen in a hole
He was so beautiful, happy and free
When he used to fly and sing from tree to tree
But then some dark fate came to call
And the hole in the snow caught his fall
He had memories of warmth and sun
Never thinking of the day his life would be done
And yet here he lies without life or breath
Here he lies in the hole where he met his death
I hope his suffering was a short one
I hope he didn't know until it was done

The Death of My Dog
(06 December 2004)

You've been my protector through all these years
You've kissed away all my fears and tears
You've kept me warm in the cold
You've always done just as you were told
You shared my bed curled up by my side
You were always one in which I could confide
Our years together have numbered many
You were always faithful like my lucky penny
But now we've both grown so very old, you see
And I don't know who'll meet death first, you or me
I'd like for us to continue on our journey forevermore
Once we're both through death's door
And live on in a kingdom of love
Surrounded by the snow-white doves
Easy, boy—don't get up—your old body is tired
You've completed the job for which you were hired
Feel my comforting touch as I softly pet you
Close your eyes and get your rest that's due
The next time you open your eyes
We will have finished our goodbyes
And soon I'll be along to run again with you
But goodnight for now—goodnight somehow

Let Me Die
(07 December 2004)

Nobody can possibly know just why
I'm not sure I can even understand
I'm past the point of wanting to try
Please bury my body beneath the land
Give my soul to God in Heaven above
I've already done my time here in Hell
I no longer feel any type of love
I've fallen too far into this deep well
There is darkness all around
It's of no use to have my eyes
Silence is my only sound
I can't even hear my own cries
Let me go now and be free
Let my soul break out and fly
Let me finally see
Let me solemnly die

I Have to Die
(07 December 2004)

I know I must be insane
The things I see are not real
My body just overflows with pain
I can't stand how bad I feel
The voices repeat in my head
I'm frightened by what they say
I can't get out of bed
I can't face this day
My anxiety is so insanely high
I'm startled by every sound
I believe it's my time to die
And have my body put underground

Loaded Gun
(07 December 2004)

A wall of darkness emerges before me
Covering up everything that I could see
The voices, the screams—all silenced
My mind becomes caught up in the violence
Suddenly, blindly, I begin to run
Looking, searching for a loaded gun
Death is chasing quickly after me
I can't avoid what's meant to be
My feet miss, I stumble and fall
From here the shadow of death is so tall
I can't find my way back to my feet
I feel like death has me beat
There to my right, within reach, I see
That treasured loaded gun waiting for me
I grasp it tightly in my right hand
And drag it back to me across the muddy land
I press the cold barrel hard against my head
And with a squeeze of the trigger I am dead
It's still silent, it's still dark, but I am calm

A Safe Place to Hide
(07 December 2004)

I stand here in a puddle of blood
While people just keep passing me by
The blood and tears escape like a flood
Nobody sees that I'm about to die
Won't somebody patch these wounds here
Won't somebody help me to heal
Won't somebody ease all my fear
Tell me that this isn't real
Stop the blood that pours from my soul
Ease all the pressure in my chest
Give me a newer, brighter goal
Hold me tight to you while I rest
Stop this pain oozing out through my skin
Bright red and bloody flowing free
My life line has become so thin
Don't let the Angel of Death take me
Keep me close by your side
And give me a safe place to hide

~

Have you ever felt the ache of empty arms or the coldness of being alone? If not, then you may not totally understand what it's like to really need a hug; but if you do know that cold, lonely, empty feeling, then this poem is for you.

~

To Be Hugged
(07 December 2004)

To be hugged must be a sweet thing
To feel somebody's love flowing through to you
To hear the soft whisper of an Angel sing
To know that their love is true
To lay my head down in your lap
To feel you gently caress my face
To drift off into a pleasant nap
To feel my heart soften its pace
To lay my head on your shoulder and cry
To feel you wipe away my tears
To know that I am loved and why
To have somebody calm all my fears
To have a human's touch so soft and sweet
I long so much to feel such a thing
To have someone that can lovingly meet
All these distant desires by hugging
To know somebody who is not afraid
To break through my armor-covered heart
To know that my emotions are not dead
To reach out and melt my cold heart
To ease my fears of any more pain
To assure me their love is true
To keep me from going totally insane
Is this something I can get from you?

Nightmares
(07 December 2004)

I'd close my eyes and sleep but I don't dare
As soon as I drift off, I slip into a nightmare
Memories of horrible things gone past
And my peaceful sleep can't ever last
Living the bad times over and over again
There's just no way to possibly win
I can never change the things that have been
Those wounds I can't ever mend
For each time I fade off to sleep
All the demons that my mind keeps
Come screaming out to haunt me
Then I wake up full of fear, you see
I'd love to have calm, peaceful dreams
But with these demons, I can't it seems

~

One night at work I overheard one of my residents cry out, "The tears are bitter!" so I wrote this poem for her even though she could never see or hear it.

~

The Tears Are Bitter
(07 December 2004)

The tears are bitter, she cried
Feeling helpless as anyone can be
The tears are bitter, she sighed
Blind and unable to see
The tears are bitter, she said
Wanting to be loved by you
The tears are bitter, she bled
Trying to lift her head
The tears are bitter
Came a lonely cry
The tears are bitter, she said
Then she chose to die

I Haven't
(07 December 2004)

Have you ever been so happy you cried?
I haven't...
Have you ever been so content you sighed?
I haven't...
Have you ever dreamed something great?
I haven't...
Have you ever gladly anticipated fate?
I haven't...
Have you ever been content with life?
I haven't...
Have you ever simply smiled at strife?
I haven't...
Have you ever been strong enough to face fear?
I haven't...
Have you ever wished your life would end here?
I have!

~

"I Am the One" is a poem for the men and women of this country that lead our young people into battle.

~

I Am the One
(07 December 2004)

I am the one that led those men
I am that one that took them into war
I am the one that taught them to defend
I am the one that led them through that door
They are the ones that didn't come back
They are the ones that died over there
I am the one that has to face that fact
I am the one that knows it's not fair
They are the ones that fought so brave
They are the ones that bled and died
I am the one that they saved
I am the one that never cried
They are the ones that lie in peace now
They are the ones that fear no more
I am the one that lives on somehow
I am the one with the guilt forevermore

Just Let Me Die
(08 December 2004)

My heart bleeds and my soul cries
My chest aches and my mind asks the whys
My knees buckle and my feet stumble
My hands shake—I am feeling so humble
I don't care to get out of bed
I don't care what has been said
Keep the sun from my eyes
Why is it everyone dies
They all leave me here alone
Not a person to hear me moan
How dare you all leave
How dare you leave me to grieve
Well, now I want to go
Now I want to know
What's on the other side
What happened to those that died
Take me out of here
Take away all my fear
Crush my lungs and stop my heart
Tear my whole life apart
Just let me die
Don't bother me with why

~

I wrote the next two poems about how I thought Dianna felt after losing Rob, how I think any mother would feel.

~

There's One Less
(08 December 2004)

I'm a mom but I'm less of one
Because I have one less son
Another Christmas is here
And it's brought with it fear
There's one less person to buy for
There's one less that'll enter my door
There's one less plate to put out
And one more reason to shout
There's one less gift under the tree
And one less to be given to me
There's one less hug to give
Because there is one less that lives
There is one less favorite dish
And one less Christmas wish
There's one less ornament to hang
And one less bell that's rang
There's one less smiling happy face
Because there's one less in the human race
There's one less bear hug
And one less cocoa mug
There's one less person near
Because there's one more Angel here.

One Less But One More
(08 December 2004)

Christmas has come around again
But it won't be the same as it has been
There's one less person here
But there's one more Angel near
There's one less light on the tree
But there's one more star that I can see
The table has one more empty chair
But there's an Angel floating there
There's one less gift under the tree
But one more reason to be happy
The tree glows unusually bright
And the star gives off a stronger light
You can feel the sadness lift around you
You can feel the comfort of the Angel so true
Yes, there is one more missing in the flesh today
But there is one more loving us in an Angel's way

Summer Is Coming
(09 December 2004)

Summer is coming
The flowers are blooming
The birds are singing
The bees are buzzing
The snow is melting
The rain is pouring
The grass is growing
It's time for mowing
The rivers are flowing
The temperatures are soaring
The kites are flying
The children are playing
The schools are closing
The boats are sailing
The beaches are filling
The wind is blowing
The trees are growing
The people are grilling
The sprinklers are running
The farmers are tilling
The gardeners are planting
The lions are roaring
The dogs are barking
And everyone's knowing
That summer is coming

The Birds
(09 December 2004)

The birds are returning from the south
The trees are growing back fresh leaves
The squirrels are running with food in their mouth
The snow melts away and the winter grieves
The birds begin building their nests
The babies won't wait very long
There's no time to take a rest
The birds begin their mating song
Soon the eggs come to be
And the parents must protect each one
When an egg hatches into a baby
The real work has just begun
Protecting them from cold and rain
Feeding each one while they grow
Their feathers they slowly gain
To help fly one day—they know
Soon the parents push them out of the nest
And teach them each to fly really high
Then the cycle starts again without rest
And only God knows why

~

"Field of Stones" is about people visiting cemeteries. For those who believe that the soul leaves the body and continues to live in some form, then I wonder why they go to a person's grave to talk to them—the only thing left there is some old bones.

~

Field of Stones
(11 December 2004)

Have you been down to the field of stones
Where the ground is full of old bones
None of the buried bodies are whole
Because none of them have a soul
Yet people come to visit these stones
That mark the burial of someone's bones
They kneel and they pray and they cry
But with the souls missing I don't know why
Don't they realize that person is gone
They took their soul and moved on along
Do you ever see them in the field of stones
Where they've buried all the old bones

~

"This Weary Soul" was written from the point of an elderly person who is bed bound and dependant on others for daily care.

~

This Weary Soul
(11 December 2004)

I lie here helpless as can be
I need you to please care for me
I can't help it when I soil the bed
And I can't eat without being fed
My hands are useless these days
I need your help in so many ways
My legs don't support me anymore
My feet are no longer able to walk the floor
My hands can't hold a brush to fix my hair
I'm no longer able to change the clothes I wear
Would you cover me up when I am cold
Help me get warm with an extra fold
I hate to ask so much of you
But would you please bathe me too
It doesn't matter how hard I try
Without you I'd never get by
Please understand when my mind lets go
And don't get flustered because I don't know
Sometimes my hearing lets me down
And I can barely hear a sound
And with these eyes I can't always see
The love you're showing to me
No, I'm no longer completely whole
But please, don't give up on this weary soul

Demon Voices
(11 December 2004)

I have this secret I keep
And it haunts me when I sleep
I never have any pleasant dreams
Because the demons are always there, it seems
They hide out in the back of my mind
Waiting for an escape to find
They haunt me all through the night
Until the first sign of light
The voices wake me all the time
There's never any reason or rhyme
I hear them as plain and loud as can be
Even though there are never any people to see
Why do they haunt me this way
What price will I have to pay
To save myself from going insane
To stop this miserable pain

~

I wrote "Losing Control" after a very stressful day at work.

~

Losing Control
(11 December 2004)

Oh God! Bless my soul!
I've had it! I'm losing control
My temper is ready to flare
I'm about to say I don't care
My jaw is clamped down tight
My hands are fists ready to fight
My breathing has picked up its pace
I feel the sweat running down my face
I'm getting a tightness in my chest
They just won't give me a rest
Make the yelling stop now
Shut up all the moaning somehow
Give me some patience right away
Bring an end to this horrible day
Calm my racing heart
Stop my mind from falling apart
Calm my temper, won't you
Fill me with peace so true

Here Again
(11 December 2004)

Once again I find myself here
Mentally overwhelmed with fear
Physically sitting in this chair
Emotionally unable to care
I feel like I just can't do it
Not even the tiniest bit
I want to scream and cry
I want to beg to know why
I need a hug so strong
Why would that be wrong
I need to feel some love from you
I need you to hold me true
Why do I feel almost insane
Why am I in this emotional pain
The tears flow ever so free
I keep thinking this can't be
I want to be a part of life
But I can't get through all this strife
Where is it—where is my gun
I have no strength left to run
I have to end it all here
I won't cry another tear

Can You Imagine
(11 December 2004)

Can you imagine no longer living
Can you imagine suddenly dying
Darkness all around keeping you from seeing
Silence all around keeping you from hearing
Can you imagine never again imagining
Never again thinking or tasting or feeling
Can you imagine your muscles, your body not moving
Can you imagine never again hurting
Never again doing any trying
Can you imagine slowly dying
Can you imagine never again needing
Running, walking or even wanting
No climbing and no fear of falling
Can you imagine finally flying
Softly, gently soaring
Can you imagine definitely dying

~

"Hero" is about the suicidal victims in the war on depression, they have fought a war that just as many will never know.

~

Hero
(12 December 2004)

They are heroes in my eyes
Even though they left so many whys
They spent years fighting a war
Their own sanity they fought for
They lived daily on the Battlefield of Life
Fighting sadness, pain and strife
They tried so hard to keep their pain hidden
They felt for some reason they had to be forgiven
They didn't want anyone to see them crying
So secretly, inside, they kept dying
They fought a war many will never know
And for that they died a hero

Rage
(12 December 2004)

The rage pulses throughout me
My heart beats hard against my chest
My blood races through my body
I need to take a little rest
My face is turning beet red
I have to pace across the floor
The rage is being rapidly fed
It's eating away at my inner core
My jaw clamped down—muscles tight
Teeth clenched and grinding
My hands are fists ready to fight
No relief anywhere am I finding
I want to scream and yell
I want to break away and run
I want everyone to know my Hell
I want them to know I'm not the only one
The tension causing me to hold in my air
The pain in my head suddenly begins
My patience is thin and beginning to wear
This is a battle nobody wins

Abort
(12 December 2004)

Aching heart
Sadness abounds
Torn apart
Emptiness without sounds
Painful back
Hurting feet
Energy I lack
Sweltering heat
A shift too long
Staffing too short
Feeling all wrong
A job to abort

Looking Down
(12 December 2004)

Up in Heaven looking down
Seeing so many wearing a frown
Crying and wailing the only sound
Sadness walking all around
A fallen little town
Completely fallen down
Heartaches by the pound
A soiled Angel's gown
Scars of pain abound
Up in Heaven looking down

Christmas Angel
(13 December 2004)

Christmas morn has come to be
And I feel an Angel waking me
A gentle kiss and whisper in my ear
Telling me I have nothing to fear
The tree seems extra colorful and bright
And there's a soft glow around the star's light
I feel a familiar touch, like a hug
And then a slight gentle tug
The fireplace is crackling and warm
And in the smoke I see my Angel's form
The love I thought I had lost
It seemed like such a high cost
But he now stands before me
Just as plain as day I can see
Down my face run the tears
Out the window went all my fears
Christmas morn has come to be
And my Angel is here with me

~

I met a friend who was told that he was facing death unless he had a certain surgery right away. Jason struggled between the desire to die and the desire to live. He didn't want to commit suicide but he didn't want to live either.

~

For Jason
(13 December 2004)

The doctor says I'm fatally ill
I have a problem that's known to kill
At first I was afraid of what would come to be
Then I was able to face my fears completely
How do I tell the people that love me
I have an illness that is deadly
How do I say, "Goodbye"
How do I say, "I want to die"
How do I say, "Don't cry for me"
How do I say, "My soul will be set free"
Will they understand just why
Will they support my decision to die
My time on this earth may soon end
There is no way possible for me to mend
I'll be flying off into space
When you look to the moon you'll see my face
I'll be there looking down on you
Watching everything that you do

A New Year
(13 December 2004)

A new year has come to be
I wonder what's in store for me
Will I live this whole year through
Will the ones I love live too
Who will be the first to die
Who will be the first to say goodbye
What will be the cause of my first tear
What will become my greatest fear
What will my greatest joy be
What will be the greatest loss I see
What kind of love will I know
Where all will I go
There are so many questions yet
And the answers are anybod's bet
I wonder what's in store
Behind time's closed door

I Know Something
(13 December 2004)

So you think you can just disappear
People will forget you were ever near
You think you can take your own life
With drugs, a gun or maybe a knife
You think nobody will ever miss you
You'll just be a statistic too
And you think anybody that does hurt
Will get over it when they put you in the dirt
You say you don't care who loves you
This life is more than you can do
You say life will go on—another day will come
People will forget you like an old piece of gum
I understand how sad you must be
And I too feel your pain intensely
But I know something you don't
I love you—and forget you, I won't
Please don't leave me here alone
Please don't leave me with just a dial tone
Please don't make me cry myself to sleep
Please don't make me hurt so deep
Please don't leave and go away
I need you to please stay

No More Need to Run
(13 December 2004)

I feel the sadness coming down
It's getting heavier by the pound
I'm too tired to get out of bed
My only wish is to be dead
I'm telling you I've had it
I can't take another bit
I want to just fade away
Never to face another day
I'm in my car speeding down the road
I'm in a careless, reckless, dangerous mode
I'm in a plane then I leap into the sky
Should I pull my chute or continue to fly
By the time they figure out my goal
It'll be too late to save this soul
At day's end, with a loaded gun
My journey will be over—no more need to run

Would You Give Up on Me
(13 December 2004)

Would you give up on me
Just open your hand and let me go
Would you pretend not to see
The good things that you know
Would you focus on the pain that I feel
And stop drying all my tears
Pretend it's impossible for me to heal
And that I'll never overcome my fears
Would you give up on me
Turn and walk quickly away
Would you try not to be
Anywhere around on that day
Would you forget you care
And just forget you know
That I ever existed anywhere
And realize that I'm ready to go
Would you give up on me
And hand me that loaded gun
Would you close your eyes so you don't see
When all the blood starts to run

Soaring High Above
(14 December 2004)

Soaring high above on Angel's Wings
Looking down at all the earthly things
I see plants live and I see plants die
I see the tides both low and high
I see the flowers bloom and fade
I see all the wondrous things God has made
I see the joy, the smiles and the cheer
And I see the frowns, the sadness and the fear
I see the people crying themselves dry
I see the emotional pain and the questions why
I see those living, dying and everywhere in between
I see the soldiers at war and the bloody scenes
I see all the things that are good and bad
I wish there was more power that I had
I soar across the sky on a current so strong
And wonder how so much became so wrong
How can I give these people a better day
How can I show them a happier way
How do I stop them from dying
How do I stop them from crying
How do I help this world that's so sad
How do I keep them from losing what they had

Written Myself Dry
(14 December 2004)

I've written myself dry
And still haven't answered why
I've explored the living and the dying
The laughing and the crying
The happy and the sad
The good and the bad
I've stood in the pouring rain
And I've touched on the insane
I've felt the warmth of the sun
And the loneliness of being the only one
I've seen the many tears
And been confused about the fears
I've written myself dry
And still don't have the answers to why

~

*There have been days recently when my job seems like it's just too
much. A part of me wants to walk right out the door, but the
responsible side of me knows better.*

~

Sinking
(14 December 2004)

I'm starting to question my choice here
Is a nursing home really where I want to be
Leaving when I should have stayed is a fear
But it's too chaotic right now for me
Call lights—three and four at a time
Residents constantly yelling out my name
Insanity quickly becoming mine
I can't handle this old game
I need a new open door
Or maybe a vacation to refresh my sanity
Is this really where I belong anymore
In the center of all their self-pity
I'm stressed out as far as I can go
I'm going to scream if they push me anymore
I'm going to go insane I know
I'm going to collapse right here on the floor
Somebody help—please take me away
Put me in a room with padded walls
Give me a shot so I can sleep for a day
I'm not accepting any phone calls
Don't ask me to make any kind of choice
Don't ask me to do any kind of thinking
Don't ask me to use my voice
Just accept that I'm quickly sinking

An Emotional Hole
(14 December 2004)

Eyes glazed over and blank looking towards me
No emotions showing in those eyes—empty as can be
A crumpled figure, motionless, sitting on the floor
No animation, no signs of life anymore
A world came crumbling down around this soul
Shocked, she's fallen into such an emotional hole
You can't bring her back from there
You can't ever again make her care
Mentally she has passed through a one-way door
Mentally she will never return again like before

163

The Sea Shore
(14 December 2004)

Hot sand between my toes
Warm water slapping against me
Seemingly washing away my woes
Then receding back into the sea
Seagulls soaring and drifting overhead
Children building sand castles, laughter in the sky
The sun drops down and the horizon turns red
Slowly the tide turns high
Sitting alone and quiet on the beach
All sadness slowly fades away
With plenty of driftwood in reach
A warm fire now ends the day

Today Is a Good Day to Die
(16 December 2004)

Today is a good day to die
The clouds are gray
The sky has begun to cry
There is no better day
The wind is blowing cold
The air is so brittle
The winter has taken hold
Life's value has become so little
Today is a good day to die
Nobody would miss me
Nobody would wonder why
They would have to let it be
They would have to understand
Today is a good day to die
To die by my own hand
In the cold bitter snow I lie
With the gun frozen in my hand
Yes, today is a good day to die
With the Christmas red seeping out onto the land
The blood soaking in and beginning to dry
Yes, today is a good day to die

It Couldn't Be You
(16 December 2004)

A loud blast rang out
A bullet rang true
Somebody gave a shout
They said it couldn't be you
It penetrated the brain
The blood flew
It started to rain
Your face turned blue
Shock on the faces all around
As you fell to your knees
Silence—there was no sound
As everybody sees
Face first you hit the ground
Blood rushing from your head
Your life is over, you are down
There is no doubt you are dead
Crying and wailing in the street
Your sanity is all gone
Your final heart beat
An Angel's song
You lie their lifeless as can be
No more enduring the pain
Loved ones clinging to thee
Others looking with disdain
You told them it would come
You warned them every day
But nobody thought you'd be the one
To take it all the way
They put your bones in the ground
But your soul drifts away
It can't ever be bound
It still lives another day

I Just Keep Giving
(17 December 2004)

I give and I give and I give
And then I find myself giving more
It's just not an easy way to live
When giving is your biggest chore
Every once in a long while
I find myself needing to take
It feels like I've come a thousand miles
Swimming all the way across the lake
I need somebody to give to me
Some love and understanding now
Before I collapse completely lonely
Can't anyone see this somehow
Nobody can give and give all the time
Without getting anything in return
Even if it's just a mere dime
Somebody has to learn

Pickles Loves Me
(17 December 2004)

My eyes are full
But the tears aren't there
Life is a bunch of bull
But I don't care
My heart feels so empty
Yet there's a ton of weight on my chest
I want to scream and yell at everybody
I just can't get any rest
I don't want anybody to call
I'm not in the mood to talk
I can feel myself as I quickly fall
I don't want any memory lane walk
I'm going to take a strong med
And get under the covers to cry
The only place I want to be is in bed
Cause I know my bird Pickles loves me

I'm Sorry
(17 December 2004)

I'm sorry to make you a victim
Of all my hurt and pain
I'm sorry to make you suffer
Because I feel I've nothing to gain
I'm sorry to make you wonder
Because I want to be alone
I'm sorry to make you hurt
Because I don't want to be on the phone
I'm sorry to make you worry
Because I want to be alone to cry
I'm sorry to make you so sad
Just because I want to die

Confusing
(18 December 2004)

Have you ever felt so misunderstood
Whatever it is you try to say
Never seems to come out the way it should
Your true emotions you can never relay
If you say this one loves me
Somebody assumes you mean nobody else does
That's not what I meant, don't you see
But it doesn't matter if that's what they believe it was
If I say nothing at all it seems
That's just as bad as saying anything
I don't get what all it means
It's just so incredibly confusing
Why can't I just hide in silence
Invisible is a good color for me
Everything has me so tense
How can I just be free

When I Need
(18 December 2004)

When I need you most you run the other way
When I have to face myself on an ugly day
It seems I only have myself to rely on
I have never faced a day alone and won
The tears eventually begin to flow
And then all my emotions finally let go
My heart aches so bad but there's no rest
With all this weight on my chest
I've bent over backwards to support you
Why can't you be there for me too
Not an "I love you," a hug or an "are you lonely?"
Just an angry note, a hang-up and a back turned on me
Why does it seem I always give so much
But when I'm in need nobody ever gives such
You can say I'm on a pity party—I don't care
It isn't going to make any difference anywhere
Say what you want and do what you do
Your excuses don't hurt me—just you

My Best of Best Friends
(18 December 2004)

I'm so sad but I know you love me
I need a hug—won't you hold me tight
I feel so incredibly lonely
Can you make my heart feel light
Will you wrap your arms around me
Can I use your shoulder on which to cry
Will you caress my face ever so gently
Will you lie beside me, my tears to dry
Will you hold me in your arms like a child
And warm me when the cold comes from within
Will you calm my emotions when they are wild
Will you be my best of best friends?

I Don't Want
(19 December 2004)

I don't want anybody to see me
I don't want them to know I'm here
I don't want anybody to talk to me
I just want to completely disappear
I don't want anybody's phone calls
I don't want anybody's mail
I don't want to stop anybody's falls
I don't want to post anybody's bail
I don't want anybody to know I'm online
I don't want anybody to know I'm out of bed
I don't want anybody to know I'm not fine
I don't want anybody to know I'd rather be dead
I don't want anybody's "good" advice to hear
I don't want anybody's helping hand
I don't want anybody's attempt to cheer
I don't want anybody to pull my head out of the sand
I don't want anybody to know that I'm awake
I don't want anybody to keep me alive
I don't want anybody to say it's for my own sake
I don't want anybody to pull me out of this dive
I don't want anybody to look and see
I don't want anybody to ask me why
I don't want anybody to try and stop me
I just want everybody to let me die

The Song I Chose
(19 December 2004)

I'm sorry you don't know what to do
I'm sorry you don't know what to say
I'm sorry you don't understand it too
I'm sorry you don't know any way
To make me feel as good as new
Or to make me enjoy the day
I sorry you don't know this doesn't only happen to you
Or know this mood does sometimes stay
Sometimes it's an effort to tie my shoe
Sometimes it's not fun to play in the hay
Sometimes I just wish I knew
How to change the clouds from a dark gray
Sometimes the reality is true
And it's a price I don't want to pay
Sometimes it doesn't matter just who
Tries to get me out of the mired clay
So please don't be overwhelmed with why
Or feel there's anything you could have changed
When I finally choose to die
Just accept that it's the song I chose and sang

The Meaning of Insane
(20 December 2004)

Can you explain to me the meaning of insane
I think that must be where I am going
Does it include a lot of mental pain
Because that is what I am now knowing
Do you hear voices that others don't
Do you scream and yell all the time
Do the voices want you to do things you won't
Do they tell you everything will be fine
Is it like you're somebody you're not
Do you find yourself in places unknown
Do you wake up in a different spot
Do you wander all through your home
Can you explain to me the meaning of insane
I think that must be where I am going
Does it include a lot of mental pain
Because that is what I am now knowing

Scrooge
(20 December 2004)

Christmas is five days away
I wish I could just sleep through the day
I don't want any gifts from anyone
I just want the season to be done
Why do I always have to smile
Doesn't anybody know I'm faking all the while
I spent money on a gift for you
Even though I didn't have the money to
I'm glad I could give it to you
Even though you probably wanted something new
I know I am the biggest Scrooge of the season
Even if I don't have any good reason

I Need
(20 December 2004)

I need to go but there is no place to run
I need to go and find me something fun
I have had it here—I am done
I cannot take another minute—not one
The stress is weighing on me like a ton
I cannot remember the last time I saw the sun
I would like to blow my brains out with a gun
But unfortunately there are none

Do You Think
(20 December 2004)

Do you think you can make me happy when I am sad
Do you think you can make me feel good when I feel bad
Do you think you can bring me up when I am down
Do you think you can make me smile when I wear a frown
Do you think you can warm my heart when it is cold
Do you think you can turn paper into gold
Do you think you can take away the pain that I feel
Do you ever believe the hurt is real
Do you understand that when I say goodbye
It is because I am going to find a way to die

Suicide
(20 December 2004)

I am very sure now that I would like to die
Even if you do not understand why
I think the best way is with a gun
If only I actually had one
I could always use a sharp knife
But that would be a painful way to end my life
I could overdose on my medications around noon
But my system is so incredibly immune
I could crash the car but that's no guarantee
The air bags may stop me from being set free
I think a rope would work mighty fine
To leave this old world far behind
At work there is a pine in the shadows so dark
Or there is the old bridges down at County Park
Yes, a rope is the method I will use
Near sunset when the sky changes its hues.

Gentle Beauty
(21 December 2004)

The sun reflects off the water, producing a blinding light
The sky with its soft clouds changes its hues
The mountains peaked with snowcaps are really a sight
Budding flowers and greening grass are some clues
High up on a current above eagles freely soar
A soft breeze makes for gentle ripples on the lake
A tall shade tree tilts toward the water a little more
The waves splash hard against the shore as they break
Moist dew drops sprinkled across the morning lawn
The gentle scent of a fresh spring rain floats in the air
All the beauty and the newness of the first dawn
All this gives you a lasting smile to wear

The Angel of Death
(21 December 2004)

Empty eyes open—
    Staring
Lungs moving—
    Barely exchanging air
Life and death balance—
    Death more tempting
Heart beats slower—
    Beats become rare
Auditory sensory heightened—
    Dying has sounds
Circulation slowing—
    Flesh turns blue
The Angel of Death abounds—
    He's come for you
Eyes open but glazed—
    Vision gone
Lungs collapsed—
    No air remains
Heart stopped—
    Death plays its song
Circulation broken—
    Blood stains
The Angel of Death takes your hand—
    The Angel of Life cries throughout the land

A Demon's Legacy
(21 December 2004)

A young woman innocent as can be
Falls victim to an ugly legacy
Her pretty ladylike ways
And her ever so happy days
Haunted by a demon of her past
A legacy that will forever last
The demons come alive in her dreams
And their voices often awaken her it seems
She is overcome with the complex fear each night
Haunted by the ugly demons of a legacy she must fight

The Angels
(21 December 2004)

There was a cry heard throughout the land
A horrible, painful wail that echoed off the sand
It was pure agony, as loud and plain as day
It was the Angel of Life seeing another soul lose its way
The waters overflowed and the land began to flood
The agonizing Angel's tears turned everything into mud
She fell to her knees with the sound of the thunder
And cried out to the Gods in agonizing wonder
"Why did I have to open my hand and let go"
"Why did the hardships of life cost me another soul"
But she knew with suicide she had no choice
The Angel of Death echoed his inviting voice
So she opened her hand of life, releasing another soul
And the Angel of Death happily took in a new foal

Voices
(21 December 2004)

Who are you
Why have you come
What do you want me to do
Where do you come from
Why can't I see you
Why don't I know who you are
Do you do what Angels do
Did you come from very far
Are you a Demon in my life
Are you the Evil in my mind
Did I create you in all the strife
Are your intentions kind
Will you show yourself to me
Will you sit by my side
Will you ever set me free
Will you ever make me hide
Can I call you when I need you
Can I send you away
When I die, will you die too
Will you be with me until that day

~

Sometimes reality is too hard to believe. It seems it's just not real. You tell yourself it must be a dream, the problem is that you can't wake up.

~

It Just Can't Be True
(21 December 2004)

No! Don't tell me he is dead
It just can't be true
Tell me that's not what you said
Tell me he made it through
I can hear his voice still
So gentle and loving to me
I can smell the cologne he wears
I can see his handsome face
I can feel my fingers in his hair
He couldn't have fallen from grace
Here's the blue shirt he likes to wear
I can feel his arms around me
He's holding me close and tight
I can feel him here by me
It just can't be right
No! He can't really be dead
It just can't be true
His car is right outside
His boots are there at the door
He just couldn't have died
Don't tell me he's gone forevermore
I know his spirit is in this room
I can feel the love of his heart and soul
He can't possibly be in a tomb
I know he's still whole
His memory is intact, you see
And it will never fade from me

Skydiving
(22 December 2004)

14,000 feet in the sky
Looking out from inside the plane
Knowing there is a chance you could die
Knowing that some think you are insane
Arms stretched out wide as you leap
Head first you leave the safety of the plane
Now you know you're in deep
You are flying—feeling no pain
This is what it's all about
This is what you jump for
At this point there is no room for doubt
Your falling towards earth at 120mph or more
The wind in your face—feeling free
Through the clouds you fall
Things on the ground becoming a reality
Time for you to make that call
Your chute opens and your flying is done
Now you float quietly, peacefully, down
It seems like you are the only one
Floating on the hem of an Angel's gown

Don't They Know
(22 December 2004)

Why is the sun out today
Why are the flowers in bloom
What's with the singing bluejay
What's with the bride and groom
Don't they know the world ended
The day you chose to die
Don't they know my heart can't be mended
Since you chose to say goodbye
What's with all the people passing me and you
What's with all the cars just speeding through
Why do they act like they never knew
Why do they all smile like they do
Don't they know the world ended
The day you chose to die
Don't they know my heart can't be mended
Since you chose to say goodbye

...For You
(22 December 2004)

I'm up here waiting—waiting for you
I'm up here watching—watching over you
I'm up on this cloud wanting—wanting you
I'm learning to fly so I can fly with you
I have Angel wings now and a pair for you
I'm up here listening—listening for you
I know you're coming—coming here too

Demon Attack
(22 December 2004)

Withdrawn from the game of life
Withdrawn from the realm of society
I'm cutting my life line with this knife
I'm no longer feeling very mighty
Curled up in the fetal position here
In a dark corner on the cold floor
Eyes filled with incredible fear
Focused on the opening door
Pail white skin drained of all blood
Trembling little being, frightened by it all
Feet covered with clay-like mud
Waiting to see what's next to fall
The door cracks open and the light bleeds in
But a shadow appears again darkening all
The Demons begin blood-curdling screaming
I'm too afraid to move at all
A Demon shoots towards me
I duck closer down to the floor
Then I open my eyes to see
The flesh has been torn
Bright red blood sprays everywhere
The pain is overwhelming as I cry
To fight back is something I don't dare
So I lie here bleeding and die

Voices Calling Me
(22 December 2004)

"Susan! Susan!" I hear the whisper of a voice say
"Wake up! You have to get up!" I quietly hear
I open my eyes, listening, afraid to look that way
"Susan! Wake up! You have to get up!"
Again fills me with fear
I quickly turn to see—but nobody is there
"Susan! Susan!" still calling out to me
I get up and search the house looking everywhere
But there are no people—the house is empty

A word here, a phrase there, music I hear
People say, "It's a passing car," or "It's the TV."
I know better—I know it's a Demon near
I can hear them even if they are something I can't see
The Demons—they haunt me night and day
Nightmares with such violence they make me sweat
The Demons grow the fears that get in my way
I wake up completely drenched, wet
Only to hear the voices calling me

191

No Place to Run, No Place to Hide
(23 December 2004)

I need to run far away
I need to run as fast as I can
I need a place where I can hide today
I don't know how much more I can stand
I turn off the lights and unplug the phone
I curl up in bed with the blankets over my head
Wishing and wanting to just be alone
If only it was as easy as it was said
It's not enough to get out of the sun
I would rather people thought I had died
But there's no place to run
And no place to hide

An Angel in Hell
(23 December 2004)

Hidden in the dark shadows of the night
Bruised, aching, swollen and bleeding
Always destined to lose the fierce fight
Thirsty, hungry, scared and needing
Some love and attention from somebody nearby
Bones broken, scarred and brittle
Doing her best to never let them see her cry
In spite of her age she is still so little
Growth stunted by such abuse over time
Darting eyes, watching, full of fear
Flesh covered in dirt and grime
God's little Angel wipes away a tear
As she huddles in a dark corner of hell.

Suicide by Pen
(24 December 2004)

I die over and over every single day
Every time I pick up the pad and pen
I commit suicide in a different way
I slip around life's crooked bend
I die by rope, knife and gun
I die suddenly and I die slow
I spend days on the run
Without any place to go
I've died in so many ways
On so many days
Under the sun's bright rays
In some way it pays
The tears are dried
And the bleeding stopped
With an Angel at my side

Christmas Is Gone
(27 December 2004)

Another Christmas is gone, faded away
Another day is done, darkness has come
The silence echoes on, there's nothing to say
I'm really missing you, my vanished loved one
I made it today, survived it somehow
I'm not certain how I ever got through
But I did and it's all over now
There's nothing left for me to do
I lie here in the stillness of the night
My mind is overcome by memories of you
Once again the lonely tears I fight
As my heart is aching, desperate for you
My arms are so empty, wanting a hug
Needing to feel your soft touch too
Look at this hole in my life you've dug
What on earth am I to do
I'm supposed to survive and live on still
As though nothing has changed in any way
But this hole in my heart I can't fill
Such a high price I've had to pay

Some Peace
(27 December 2004)

My life has reached its night
There's no reason left to fight
The day seemed to be so long
And everything in it so wrong
But now I sit here in the dark
Looking for any little friendly spark
Something good to light my way
And get me through another day
But as the silence echoes true
All I can think of is you
And I think I'd like to die
Without anybody asking me why
I'd like to be at your side
And never have emotions to hide
I want to escape this world somehow
And find some peace now

~

Tomorrow is Christmas Eve, and I should be full of the Christmas spirit—but I'm not. I often ask myself, "Will it ever get better?" and I know it will, but at that moment I can't see it, I can't feel it, I can't remember it and I can't believe it. I ask myself what keeps me here on this earth, in this life that I see as being rather miserable at the moment, and I don't really know. I can think of things to get me through to the next minute, and sometimes that is all I have to go on but it works. Once again another year has come to a close, and I ask myself how I ever made it this long—maybe that is what keeps me going for another year, maybe it's the one minute at a time. I know I owe a great deal to my psychologist, who just keeps handing the credit back to me, but the truth is if she had not been there to help me work through these things I would not be where I am today. I'm sure she would argue that point, but I hope somewhere deep down she understands how important she has been in my life. Maybe if she went away today I would be okay for the next ten years, but it would only be because of what she has taught me in the last ten years. There is nothing to get you through life like a great psychologist.

Merry Christmas and Happy New Year to each of you!!

The next poem is about losing somebody that you love so much they are like a part of you.

~

Somebody Cut My Arm Off
(01 January 2005)

Somebody cut my arm off, I don't know why
I turned my back for a minute and now I want to die
I used that arm so much and now it isn't here
Somebody cut my arm off and now I'm full of fear
Somebody took you away, you were a part of me
I closed my eyes for a minute and now I can no longer see
I needed you so much and now you're gone
Somebody took you away and now everything is wrong
How can I do this alone without you at my side
I've been so lost ever since the day that you died
You were always there for me way back when
But now I know that without you I can never mend
Somebody took you far away from here
And now I have no arm to wipe away my tear

~

"Run with the Wind" is a poem that will only be fully understood by Rob, his mom and me.

~

Run with the Wind
(03 Jan 2005)

Do you know what it means to run with the wind?
Do you know what this means, my friend?
When times are tough and you can't get through,
Take my hand and I'll run with the wind and you.
When the sky seems dark and the thunder rolls,
When you feel like you're being raked over the coals,
When all your hope seems to be lost
And you don't think you can pay the cost,
When you just don't know exactly what to do,
Take my hand and I'll run with the wind and you.
This is our secret, nobody knows
Exactly how the old tale goes.
But there is one in heaven above,
Who is pure as the snow-white dove,
That makes the gentle wind blow
And the corn stalks grow
So that you and I, my friend,
Can run with the wind.

It's Snowing
(05 January 2005)

The cold snow keeps coming down
Turning things white all around
It piles up on the streets and walks
A man outside turns white as he talks
All the dirt and grime of this land
Is turned white with a sweep of God's hand
The tree branches bend beneath the snow's weight
It keeps building until the branches finally break
The squirrels hibernate in their trees
While most of the ground is in a deep freeze
The lakes and ponds are all iced
And the skaters are all enticed
They bundle up as warm as they can
And go out to play on the frozen land
The crystal flakes reflect the light
On this crisp, full moon night
And the winter's beauty is at its best
While we sit near the fire and rest

~

Again, I felt the need to write a poem for Dianna about the loss of her child.

~

Flesh of Your Flesh
(05 January 2005)

As a newborn babe, God gave me to you.
I was born flesh of your flesh to do as you do.
Under your gentle, loving wing I grew,
How I would turn out, nobody knew.
Often my heart was broken in two
And my body changed from when it was new.
You often prayed to the God from which I came
To help me win at life's twisted game.
But then one day I decided I was a man
And wanted to explore some new land,
So out from under your wing I ran
And sailed throughout the land.
Soon the Devil took a hold of my soul
And drug me to the bottom of a black hole.
There I was, blood of your blood,
Lying face down in the filthy mud,
Then God above felt your heart's pain
And flooded my life with a cleansing rain.
Although you can't understand why,
God decided to let me die.
But despite of all my angry ways,
He forgave me for all my life's days.
He mended my broken soul
As he lifted me from that deep hole.
Now I am the Angel you hear and see
That keeps you always thinking of me.

Dreams and Nightmares
(07 January 2005)

Dreams that pass me by in the night
Nightmares that fill me full of fright
Things unseen except for a flare
The only way I'm ever aware
A flare in the corner of my eye
But then vanished after it's gone by
I turn my head toward it to see
But it's already flown on past me
My dreams, my nightmares, all the same
The good and the bad all wearing my name
It doesn't matter if I'm asleep or awake
It's all more than I can take
There isn't any rest for my soul
There isn't any way out of this hole
My dreams pass me by unseen
What does it all really mean
Nightmares take over my sleep
Causing me to continually weep
Dreams fading at the break of day
There never seems to be any other way
Fading flares in the corner of my eye
Memories of days gone on by

~

*I'm not sure if I wrote this poem about committing suicide or
just dying.*

~

I'll Wade
(09 January 2005)

My heart is aching, broken and bleeding
My body is bruised, hurting and needing
My soul is splintered and painfully hollow
This isn't the path I wanted my life to follow
A single set of footprints in the snow
Exactly where they lead nobody knows
Over the horizon they shrink and fade away
Never to return on another day
A broken heart, bruised body, splintered soul
A person that believes they'll never be whole
It seems that life isn't worth living
And that death can be very giving
When a choice must finally be made
Through the muddy waters to death I'll wade

~

*Have you ever had one of those days when you feel really old?
What of the young, do they ever think of what life will be like when
they are old?*

~

It Will Come to Me
(10 January 2005)

I hope that when I come to death's door
I can say, "I don't want for one thing more."
So many years, didn't they go by in a blink?
Life's chain joined together with each link
I've seen so much more meaning in my life
Than I've ever had any reason to expect
The image becomes sharper than a pointed knife
An image that nobody can ever take from me
When my time comes to leave and be free
I want to say that I have no regrets of any kind
And that I'm not afraid of what I'm yet to find
I know I'm old—I'll always be old
Life is something that we should gently hold
But now death's door is very near to me
And yet, through it, I still can't see
And so what should I do now—
I guess it will come to me somehow

Listen to Me
(12 January 2005)

Listen to me won't you please
Hear me—my pain you could ease
There is so much that I want to say
Before I face one more day
Listen to me won't you please
I'm lost, floating on open seas
Can't you hear what I'm trying to say
All the words just get in the way
Can you see the emptiness inside of me
Can't you hear me trying to be free
My hearts seems so lonely and hollow
I'm searching for a ray of sunshine to follow
Just listen to me, won't you please
Hear me—my pain you could ease

~

Every September in Kokomo, Indiana, there is a veterans reunion. The turnout is magnificent and I've made it there the past few years. It is always a fun and educating experience to be around this countries heroic veterans.

~

Kokomo, Indiana
(18 January 2005)

A gathering of old soldiers reliving still fresh pain
They come every year regardless of the cold or rain
They've come together to share the secrets of their soul
Respect, gratitude and brotherhood is their very goal
The old wounds stir again, bringing back all the pain
This is the only place where they know they're not insane
They tell their tales of the good and bad times gone by
And remember the faces of those that had to die
So that they themselves could live to see another day
And they're still wishing there could have been another way
All of these men have similar memories to share
And they know that this is where people care
Their tears fall like rain laying down the dust
Clearing the air, making way for some new trust
Soldiers in each other's arms, standing tall
Not one ever hears the bartender's last call
Arm in arm they raise the mighty flag of this land
Eye to eye, their tears wash away the man
Old soldiers full of such aching pain
Old soldiers trying to stay sane

My Beam of Light
(18 January 2005)

Slashing, cutting, crossing through the darkness
Pulling back the very covering of its heart
Singling out each corner, revealing the loneliness
Ripping the dark shadows of the night apart
My little beam of light complementing the moon and stars
Slowly, silently, I creep through the dark night
Keeping one eye on the distant red planet, Mars
Acknowledging each little thing that comes into sight
The dark night identical to a sadness within me
My little light is the mind searching for a way out
Trying harder and harder for some happiness to see
Attempting to figure out what all this is about
Whatever you do, don't turn out my little light
Help me to find the sun's brilliant, warm rays
Push away the darkness forever from my sight
And keep my path lit throughout the days

He Was Here
(20 January 2005)

He was here with me for so very long
Then he vanished suddenly from sight
He took with him life's sweet song
As he disappeared into the dark night

He left me with a broken, shattered heart
He left me here gasping for air
He left me here with a missing part
A part of my soul—like he didn't care

What am I to do without him here
What am I to do now that he's gone
What am I to do with each little tear
What am I to do without his sweet song

How could he have just left without care
How could he have thrown away my love
I know that life isn't always fair
But I feel like a broken-winged dove

He was here with me for so very long
Then he vanished suddenly from sight
I'm telling you—this is so very wrong
Nothing about this can ever be right

Which One
(20 January 2005)

Reds, yellows and oranges span the summer sky
A silhouetted figure silently standing on the beach
Wondering how, asking himself over and over why
Sadness is never ending, happiness never within reach
Is the horizon's light rising or falling out of sight
The bright, sunlit day bringing an ever so sweet peace
But only dark shadows are present within the night
Loneliness, emptiness, sorrow and pain that won't cease
The depths of the darkness portraying death for me
The brightness of the sun portraying life at its best
Which one will I choose to forever be
Which one will give my heart a rest

I Wish
(24 January 2005)

I wish I had the balm to soothe your pain
I wish I had the umbrella to shelter you from the rain
I wish I had the blanket to keep you warm when it's cold
I wish I had the fountain to make you young when you're old
I wish I had the tools to mend your broken heart
I wish I had a way to give you a new start
I wish I was an angel that protected you from harm
I wish I could protect you with a sweep of my arm
I wish I could make all your hurt go away
I wish I could put the sun in your every day
But I am only able to love you
And hope that it will be enough to do

~

Today is the six-month anniversary since Rob decided his own fate. Six months seems like an eternity in some ways and like only yesterday in others.

~

Six Months
(24 January 2005)

Six months of sadness and sorrow
Six months of happiness I've had to borrow
Six months of roaming around in the night
Six months of knowing you're gone from sight
Six months of loving you—lost
Six months of knowing the cost
Six months of my world pale and blue
Six months of my life without you
Six months since you chose to die
Six months since I started asking why
Six months since my world bottomed out
Six months of nothing but doubt
Six months since you locked the door
Six months since time became no more
Six months since you said goodbye
Six months—I remember—then sigh

~

I have a Congo African Grey named Smokey, and I wrote this poem in hopes of teaching him to some day recite it.

~

Smokey
(27 January 2005)

My name is Smokey
I came from an egg
I'm never pokey
And I sleep on one leg
I like to entertain you
Make you laugh when I can
I can do everything you do
And I am my greatest fan

Acupressure
(28 January 2005)

Would you take hold of my hand
And hold it the special way that you do
Take me to a faraway land
A land where there's just us two
Would you show me the soft playing band
Let me hear the gentle music too
Would you take hold of my hand
And hold it the special way you do
Would you walk through the warm sand
As the sun sets with colors so true
Would you give me the peace I know you can
And ease my pain the way that you do?

That Would Be Fine
(28 January 2005)

You ask me how I am mentally
I tell you that I am confused
You ask me how I am physically
I tell you that I am abused
You ask me how I am emotionally
I tell you that I am sad
You ask me how I am spiritually
I tell you that it's bad
You sigh and turn to walk away
Unknowing of what to do
I ask, "Don't you have anything to say?"
You simply state, "I can't help you."
Your shoulders droop and your tears run
Your sad eyes lock in with mine
I show you my loaded gun
And you say, "That would be fine.
Let's leave this world, you and I,
Let's find a better life around the bend.
It is our time to die.
There's no chance for us to mend."
Your frown shadows mine
And I say, "That would be fine."

Blue Hue
(28 January 2005)

There's too much blue in my world today
And I don't know how to change the hue
There's sadness all around me, they say
And I just don't know what else to do
I tried crayons, markers, paint and dye
But none of it would ease this blue mood
I just don't know what else to try
How do I make this sadness understood?

I Began to Mend
(29 January 2005)

A sadness came and overwhelmed my soul
It seeped slowly in until it filled the hole
It snuffed all of the candles' flames out
As the darkness turned everything into doubt
It changed my entire world's hue
To a saddened shade of deep blue
I found I had a deep desire to write
It seemed the only way to survive the night
So I found my paper and pen
And I began to mend

~

Dianna said one day that she was afraid of Rob coming into her dreams, she didn't know if she could handle it because sometimes our dreams are so real to the mind that you wake up and think it really happened. I wanted her to understand that seeing Rob in her dreams would be a good thing.

~

Come into My Dreams
(31 January 2005)

I wish you would come into my dreams
I've waited so very long, it seems
It's been months since you went away
I'll never forget that fateful day
I long to see you and touch you again
A soothing moment for my heart to mend
Won't you come to visit with me
Won't you step out of Heaven and be free
Float, my Angel, into my dreams
Be that shining star that gleams
Every night while I lie in my bed
Thinking of you in my head
Won't you please come to this place
Let me once again touch your face
Let me once again feel your touch
I miss it so very, very much
Let me hold you in my arms tight
Maybe this time I can keep you in sight
Step out of Heaven, my sweet Angel
Come visit me in this earthly Hell
Slip into my dreams just for a time
Let me touch you, sweet Angel of mine

~

One of the painful things in the grief process is wondering if you will ever forget the one you lost. You want to treasure every bit of their memory forever, but the reality is that without photos and such our memories do fade with time. I hope I never forget what Rob looked like, talked like, walked like or his sense of humor.

~

His Face Is Gone
(31 January 2005)

My memory has begun to fail me
The years have become so many
The image of him is fading fast
I thought it would forever last
But now, it seems, his face is gone
And I've lost his voice's sweet song
I can still see an image of his being
I know it's his body I'm seeing
But I can't see his face anymore
It's passed beyond my memory's door
What do I do now that his face is gone?

Mystery
(02 February 2005)

There's a mystery out there—uncharted land
Oceans of water and beaches of sand
There are places I haven't yet been
And flowers I still need to tend
There are mountains I've yet to climb
And memories that are not yet mine
There are valleys yet to walk through
And streams yet to wade too
There are lakes I still want to see
And white water rafts waiting for me
There are corners I've not rounded
And bells I've not yet sounded
There are still mysteries out there
Of that much I am aware

Angel of Mine
(03 February 2005)

I can feel his tender loving touch at night
As he holds me in his Heavenly arms so tight
I can hear the soft flutter of his wings
And his gentle voice comforts me when he sings
The darkness is no longer a thing to fear
Whenever I know that he is near
My aching heart is softer since the day he died
Because I know that he is by my side
The tears that once flowed like a gentle rain
Are gone at this moment with all the pain
I feel his hand gently caress my face
As my heart slowly softens its pace
His bright, shining halo lights my way
And it is my sun on a stormy day
My sadness is eased for a moment in time
When I can feel this Angel of mine

Time
(03 February 2005)

The time has come now for me to go
Don't ask me how it is that I know
It's just something that I can feel within me
It's not something that you could ever see
My time here needs to finally end
It's time for me to round another bend
I'm glad that I've known you while I was here
But now the time for me to die is drawing near
It's time to say goodbye, my dear friend
Don't cry for me when the pain I finally end
To a great land of peace is where I'll go
I'll be so much better then—I know
I'll send you an Angel from Heaven above
To remind you of my undying love

~

I wrote the following poem after a session with Dr. Jump, our time always seems so short. Have you ever wished your therapist could be there anytime day or night, sometimes it's hard to wait until you have an appointment and then still be able to express the same emotions.

~

Time and Emotions
(04 February 2005)

The clock is ticking—time is passing us by.
The emotions are there but I can't find a way
To put them into words or to tell you why
I'm crying so many tears on this day.

The pain is sharper than a kitchen knife,
It pierces my very soul from within,
It measures my every moment in life
And keeps count of my every sin.

Tick, tick, tick, the clock moves on ahead—
Time slowly passing us by, a minute, an hour,
Counting the living and the mounting dead
Like the unfolding and wilting of a flower.

What words do I use to make you see
The mounting torment and the stabbing pain?
How do I make you feel what's inside of me,
How do I make you see I've nothing to gain?

Tick, tick, tick, the clock moves on ahead—
The days come and the days go one by one.
I often wonder why I even get out of bed,
Everything I can do has already been done.

Watch the hand on the old grandfather clock
As it moves so slow, a minute at a time,
Slowly I hear the doors beginning to lock
This life, this period of time is no longer mine.

The emotions finally begin to fade by and by,
The words still are not there for me to say,
The tears have finally begun to dry—
But the clock ticks on for another day.

~

Dr. Jump talked about how we carry things around. Problems are like rocks, we pick them up and put them in our backpack until finally the load is so heavy we can't carry it anymore. Talking out problems are like removing rocks from your load.

~

Stone by Stone
(06 February 2005)

I come to you often, my burdens to unload
Stone by stone, I give each one to you
Together we travel down a long, stony road
You help me figure out what's best to do
When our time is up I walk slowly away
Leaving most of my stones behind with you
I collect new stones with the passing day
So that I can unload them when they are due
You accept each of my stones one by one
And when you think the time is right
You open my eyes to show what's been done
And I can't hardly believe what's in sight
My tears no longer have a need to run
You've taken each stone that I gave
And built a bridge under the sun

Melting Pot
(06 February 2005)

Dreams, goals, success and defeat
Throw them in a pot and fire up the heat
Add broken hearts, confusion and sadness
Don't forget to add in a little happiness
Turn up the heat and stir the pot
When it's all mixed in, see what you've got
A life, a story, emotions by the load
Experience walking beside you down the road
Tears that have flowed and tears that have dried
You'll see many that lived and many that died
A cycle from birth to death known as living
A reason for life itself known as giving
A reason for death still rather unknown
A child victim of life now all grown

~

Ever watch the news and get depressed at what's happening in our very own world, maybe wanting to help but not knowing where to start or if we could even make a difference?

~

Eternity
(07 February 2005)

It's like our world is coming to an end
That eternity is just around the bend
Wars and battles abound worldwide
People everywhere with a gun at their side
Rape, murder, suicide, killing of all kinds
Changing morals and beliefs in our mind
Terrorist attacks occur more and more
Every day we move closer to Hell's door
God being removed from our government
Young soldiers dying everywhere they are sent
To defend our country from the feared enemy
While every day more people enter into poverty
Jobs lost—sent to places far away from here
Americans once free, now living in deep fear
Yes, I believe our world is coming to an end
And that eternity is just around the bend

A Relentless Thing
(08 February 2005)

Grief is such an ongoing, relentless thing
Weighing down our painful, broken hearts
Like alcohol on a wound, it continues to sting
Tearing our fragile lives completely apart
It seems like it nests somewhere in our soul
Dragging us deeper and deeper into a hole
Rooting itself incredibly deep and strong
Reminding us of how everything is so wrong
It darkens the very light by which we see
Causing us to stumble and fall repeatedly
It blinds us of anything good that's yet to be
And never gives us an answer to the why
Days, months and years pass us by
And still the pain lingers on so near
Filling us full of a dark, dark fear
And flooding our eyes with lonely tears
That never really seem to dry

~

Sometimes we believe that a person's suicide must have been a mistake, they would never really leave us behind on purpose, something must have gone wrong for them to be dead.

~

Was It a Mistake
(10 February 2005)

How do I know that you ever loved me
Why didn't you trust me to help you
Were you sheltering me from what was to be
Or were you thinking that I already knew
How long had you been planning to leave
When did you make your decision to go
What a tangled web of hurt you did weave
There's so many answers I don't know
Was it a mistake that went too far
Did you really intend to actually die
Now what do I do with your car
How do I explain to everybody why
Your room is just the way you left it
Your toothbrush sits now all alone
There's an empty chair where you once did sit
Your dog still lies and waits for you to come home
Your favorite magazines still come in the mail
Your bow and gun gather more dust each day
And I sit looking at your fishing pail
Wondering why you had to die this way

I Want to Die
(10 February 2005)

I have a deep desire to just say goodbye

What reason is there to stay alive
All life's problems seem to constantly multiply
No denying I'm in a fast dive
Today is worse than yesterday

There's never any happiness for me
Others have tried to show me the way

Does my existence really have to be
Isn't there any happiness near
Even a little to calm my fear

Blind Am I
(10 February 2005)

Blind am I—I cannot see
This reality has always been for me
I've never seen myself in a reflection
I've never made a color selection
I've never seen the sky so blue
I've never seen the likes of you
I've never seen my mother's face
I've never seen a horse race
I've never seen my father's eyes
I have so many unanswered whys
I've never seen the sun or the moon
I've never seen a clock at high noon
I've never seen the early morning dew
Or even the evening sky's hue
I've always wondered about the stars
And the evolution of the cars
I'd like to see the ocean's waves
And my family's ancient graves
But blind am I—I cannot see
This reality has always been for me

Dawn
(11 February 2005)

Morning glory peeking over the horizon
Colors of red and orange in the sky
Look fast before it's completely gone
Don't worry about the unanswered why
Beauty at its finest before me
Peace at its best inside
All this beauty for us to see
No reason for anyone to hide
Colors reflecting off the lake
The sun warming my face
Slowly the day comes awake
Revealing all of its grace

~

Eventually we all must reach a point where we have to accept it did happen, it was their choice, we couldn't have stopped it forever and now we must live with the decision they made to die.

~

I'll Never Know Why
(11 February 2005)

I have to accept this choice you made
Even though it hurts so terribly bad
Unknowingly, I watched your candle fade
I wish that I had seen that you were so sad
I look at you now in this box of wood
As I stand here and softly weep
You look so peaceful, I knew you would
Your eyes closed as though you are asleep
Your demons are now gone forevermore
Eternal peace is finally yours to keep
I know you passed through Heaven's door
I know you will never again weep
But I am still here drowning in sorrow
I don't know why this choice you made
And I still won't know tomorrow
All the sadness you had to wade
All the tears you had to cry
All the demons you had to face
I guess I'll never know why

Make Words Rhyme
(11 February 2005)

Can you teach me how to make words rhyme
Can you show me exactly how to capture time
Can you teach me how to write tears down
Can you teach me a good way to use a noun
Can you teach me how to make others see
All the pain that's stuck down inside of me
Can you teach me how to pass along
That I can no longer sing a happy song
So many times and so many ways
I've tried to show them the way
But no matter how hard I tried
I just couldn't relay what was inside
My chest hurts from my swollen heart
My life is all broken apart
The tears washed my smile away
I don't want to go on another day
But I don't know how to write tears down
Or how to make you see my frown
Can you teach me how to make words rhyme
Can you show me exactly how to capture time

~

The poem "Mama's Baby Boy" was written for my Congo African Grey one day as I watched him watching me.

~

Mama's Baby Boy
(11 February 2005)

Quietly, quizzically perched on his door
Watching me, wondering what for
"Hello," he says, waiting for a reply
"Give Mama kiss," he says, standing by
Fluffing his feathers, bobbing his head
Repeating things that have been said
"I love you," I softly say as I smile
"I love you," he says, waiting all the while
I rub his head and kiss him on the beak
"Yeehah!" he says back with a shriek
"Mama's baby boy," I gently say
As together we start a new day

Written for Smokey

Emotions of Every Kind
(12 February 2005)

Confusion, frustration, anger, emotions of every kind
No peace, no calm, no happiness will I ever find
Chest aching, tears building, anxiety is too high
Soon I can't hold it in anymore and I cry
I want to give up, hide, say a final goodbye
My feet stumble and I fall, unable to walk
The words are gone, my tongue tied, I can't talk
Thoughts racing through my mind way too fast
All these horrible memories from my past
The only way to stop these demons is to die
And that's just exactly what I would try
But there is a distant flame in my view
A light as gloriously bright as when it was new
A small candle in the corner of my eye
Dancing in the wind, struggling to survive
It's my little light of hope, my only one
When it is finally snuffed out, I am done
And that will be the last time I cry
As I take a desperate stand and die

The Dead of the Night
(16 February 2005)

The sun sets low in the sky
Darkness is creeping upon us fast
Soon all the colors will fade and die
I don't know how long the dark will last
My candle once burned so very low
Now the flame is gone—it burns no more
Time seems to be moving by slow
I can't see the Heaven's doors
I'm in between Heaven and Hell
Caught among the living dead
And I don't understand how I fell
I don't know what's going on in my head
Fearsome cries in the dead of the night
Dark shadows hunting me down
Paralyzed and full of fright
I can't handle the screaming sounds
I feel the warm blood oozing down
The pain is more than I've ever known
It seems that peace can never be found
It can't ever be heard above the moan

Can You
(17 February 2005)

Can you silence the world and slow my heart
Can you ease my pain and calm my fear
Can you touch me and give me a new start
Can you turn back the clock to a better year
Can you hold me and tell me everything is okay
Can you take away the demons in my mind
Can you erase all the evil in some way
Can you help me with some true love to find
Can you stop all the bleeding in my soul
Can you erase all of the scars that are within
Can you carry me to my final goal
Can you please help me to mend

To Be...
(17 February 2005)

To be touched—striking a warmth within
To be seen—triggering a shy grin
To be hugged—the true squeeze of love
To be held—feeling safe like the Angels above
To be spoke to—to hear another's kind word
To fly free—to feel like a flighted bird
To be thought of—to know somebody does care
To be loved—do I dare?

Meds
(18 February 2005)

I don't want to take my meds anymore
I no longer wish to pass through that door
My happiness isn't real, it's fake
And I've taken about all I can take
The real me has far more emotion
More pain and tears mixed in the potion
I want to feel everything again
I want to go back to where I've been
I want to express myself in a new way
Even if it means doubting myself each day
Without my meds I'm full of fear
Because I know that suicide is near
But those very thoughts of fear, you see
Can also bring comfort to me
I don't want to take my meds anymore
Unless they can give me the freedom to soar
High above all the clouds in the sky
So high I never wonder why

Twenty Years Ago
(18 February 2005)

Twenty years ago I was only seventeen
And there was so much I hadn't yet seen
I was young, healthy, pretty and naïve
The world still held more than I could conceive
It was a time before I ever saw foreign land
A time when innocence was still close at hand
A time of setting goals and shooting for dreams
A time when the world was so big, it seemed
School lay behind me, life lay ahead
There was never thought of the living or dead
Still a child caught in an adult's body somehow
Wondering what I should do now
That was just about twenty years ago
When there was still so much I didn't know
To turn the clock back would be a magical thing
To be flying gently along on time's wing
Reliving the good, erasing all the bad
Thinking more clearly about the choices I had
Changing my fate in every way
Changing who I am today

This Place
(20 February 2005)

In my journey through life
There is so much strife
And I have come to a place
Where there was once a loving face
But now there is a large hole
An emptiness that tugs at my soul
It's a dark place of pain
Where all my crying is in vain
That face is gone forever now
And I must live alone somehow
But I can't ease the pain in my heart
I can't handle falling apart
I can't stop the tears
Or calm all of my fears
Since I came to this place
This deep, dark, lonely space
Where love used to be
Where my heart is now empty

Peace
(20 February 2005)

Make everyone and everything go away
Give me that sacred feeling of peace today
Lift the weight off my shoulders and ease the pain
Erase from my mind all the blood stain
Mend my heart and restore my soul
Pull me out of this cold, empty hole
Return all the sacred loves I've lost
Wipe away all the consequences and cost
Set me on top of a mountain so high
Set me up above the clouds in the sky
Let me see the sun rise and set
And erase every penny of my debt
Give me a true and meaningful peace
Make all of my pain cease

~

I have found through the years that I cannot write unless I am sad about something, so I have not been taking my medication lately like I should. The downside is dealing with the emotions, some days are hard, but the upside is that I can write. However, the time has come for me to give up the struggle, lay down my pen and pick up my medication once again.

~

Until We Meet Again
(27 December 2004)

This book has now come to an end
It's time for me to lay down my pen
And to put my pad of paper off to the side
Since most of my tears have dried
It's time to bring this book to a close
Until once again the pain grows
On this day I don't wish to die
Or to tell everyone goodbye
I wish you all the best life has to give
And the ability to escape sadness so you can live
May you find enough happiness in each day
To carry you through on your way
And now until we meet again
I've officially put down my pen

~

Life is poetry in motion and poetry goes on. It goes beyond the words, beyond the pages, beyond the chapters and beyond the books. Like life goes on beyond the graves, it continues in our photos, our diaries, our videos and our memories.

In closing I ask you this question: is the pain we feel over losing one we love worth all the joy they gave us when they were here in our world? If we choose to lose the pain, then we would also be choosing to lose the love, the joy, the memories, the treasured moments, the sunrises and sunsets we shared with them.

~

Printed in the United States
33856LVS00004B/335

9 781413 781779